Creatively WIN Workbook

JUMPST★RT
YOUR WRITING
IN
30 DAYS

A Step-By-Step Guide to Becoming a More Productive Writer

Heather Kelly

Creatively WIN by jumpstarting your writing habit now! From the founder of the Writers' Loft, this workbook sets you up to win your writing goals, starting today. The bite-sized exercises, thoughtful inspirations, and useful tools within its pages pave the way to a more productive, more creative, healthier you. Don't write alone--

Cover design by TeaBow Studio
Book interior design by Robert Thibeault

Also by Heather Kelly

POETRY ANTHOLOGIES

Firsts

An Assortment of Animals
Friends and Anemones

Look for These Upcoming Books:

NONFICTION WORKBOOKS
Creatively WIN--Jumpstart Your Drafting in Thirty Days
Creatively WIN--Jumpstart Your Revision in Thirty Days

YA FICTION
(Written as HG Kelly)
Blindspot
Soul Searching

TWEEN and MG FICTION
Maybe I Should Drive

Contents

Introduction

We all want to win. At writing, at life; at every endeavor we take on. Our biggest and only competitor in the writing game is our own selves. We live in our heads to create stories and don't always pay attention to the barriers preventing us from being creative and productive.

WHAT DOES IT MEAN TO WIN AT WRITING?

It means knowing **What I Need** at any given point. Get it? **WIN**. Every writer, at every stage in their career, needs something. This workbook will help you figure out what you need and help you get it.

Winning also means making the process fun and sustainable!

WHY SHOULD THIS WORKBOOK (AND I) BE YOUR GUIDE?

The road to success becomes easier and better when you have a blueprint, daily progress and accountability, and tools to combat anxiety, self-doubt, and the emotional pitfalls of the creative process.

Through this workbook, I'll be your guide. In fact, I'll be your "first follower." Go ahead, search, and watch Derek Sever's video First Follower Leadership Lessons—I'll wait, it's worth it! The video talks about leaders and followers, which translates into writers and their fans as well. Let me be your first follower, the one who tells you that you are not a "lone nut," and help you build momentum in your writing career.

Throughout the upcoming sections, there will be more opportunities to watch videos, listen to podcasts, and allow experts to teach you. Let them. Trust this process and take advantage of every avenue to learn. Take deeper dives when you feel particularly interested in the topic at hand. Put your whole self in.

This workbook evolved out of my most popular workshops given at writing conferences, and from my twenty years of coaching writers and helping them get their stories into the hands of fans.

I've studied all different types of professional writers—traditionally published authors under deadlines, successful indie publishers paving their own way, and work-for-hire authors committed to the side hustle. I've produced conferences for writers and built a thriving local writing community from the ground up, giving a ton of thought to what a creative person needs to produce their intellectual property.

I don't ask anyone to do anything I don't do. I walk the walk myself. I've written books, revised books, critiqued books, edited books, and published books.

And now, I'm sharing what I've learned with you.

You'll find a few steadfast tenants or themes throughout the book: Strive to keep learning, there's no need to reinvent the wheel, and work smarter; not harder.

The work you do within these pages will put you in the best place to WIN at your creative projects going forward.

Bottom Line:
You Can do This!

HOW TO USE THIS WORKBOOK:

Pledge to jumpstart your writing over the next thirty days. Every day you plan to write, open this workbook and follow its directions. It's that easy.

The first six days of this manual are prep. On day seven, you'll carve out writing time before working through the day's activity. Feel free to go as quickly as you want through the first six sessions, but once you start writing, try to do one session each day to preserve your writing time. This workbook will be with you each day you are writing.

This workbook is set up as if you are starting a new creative project, but works just as well if you are in the middle of a manuscript. Just give yourself the space to pause your project to plan and think about your goals and writing future. Remember, there is no wrong way to use this workbook. It is here to support you and help you become a more productive writer.

If you happen to skip a day of planned writing, skip to Section Thirty-one, You've Missed A Day. It'll help you analyze the barrier to writing and how to get over it.

In the Appendix, you'll find extra copies of the worksheets so you can repeat parts of the process. That way, when you finish this workbook and your current project, you can use this workbook again and again as your blueprint for success.

Are you ready to **WIN?!**
Let's get to it!

Author's Thank You Note: I will mention my gratitude for some of my author friends throughout this book. I hope you appreciate them too and what they bring to this workbook. If you do, check out their creative projects. Let my posse becomes your posse! Thank you, author **Pam Vaughan**, for showing me that brilliant first follower video and for being the first and most enthusiastic follower for me and the Writers' Loft community!

IDEA ORCHARD

Day 1 Task: WIN at brainstorming.

CHECK-IN:
We'll do this each day. It's important to take our creative temperature so we know when we need to feed the well.

Rate yourself on this scale:

Not excited   **0 1 2 3 4 5 6 7 8 9 10**   Totally excited

Tip: If you check in with yourself and don't feel excited about creating, find a way to get there! Take a walk, listen to music, bake—do something to get you in the creating mood. If you don't have time to psych yourself up, then set your mind to work through the creative dip. We'll take a deeper dive into filling the creative well on Day Thirteen.

Here's another scale to rate:

Not focused   **0 1 2 3 4 5 6 7 8 9 10**   Totally focused

Tip: Sometimes we can't focus because we have a ton on our mind. I keep a running list of to-dos beside my computer and jot things down when they interrupt my writing focus. Once down on a list, I can let them go. I may never get to all those to-dos, but at least they aren't rolling around in my mind becoming irritants.

Welcome to the process! I'm glad you're here. Each day in this workbook, you'll have at least one simple activity to WIN and on day seven you'll WIN at carving out writing time as well!

TODAY'S ACTIVITY TO WIN: IDEA ORCHARD

You've probably started this manual with a project that you've committed to in your mind. There's a lot of value to taking a step back and brainstorming all the projects that you are thinking about doing at one point or another.

Why do people talk about idea gardens? It's because we have lots of ideas and need a place to plant them. It'll free up your brain space once those ideas are in a safe place.

Here we're talking about an Idea Orchard, because I want you to think about your ideas in a larger sense. Those ideas start as seeds that grow into trees and produce fruit. The fruit will have other idea seeds inside, which you can then plant. Every idea taken to fruition (pun intended!) will give you next-level ideas for you to follow.

Flip to **Worksheet 1: WIN at Creating Your Idea Orchard** and brainstorm onto it all the projects relating to writing that you are considering. Don't hold back; nobody is going to judge you on your ideas. Get your ideas out. Every last one. They could be writing-adjacent projects, like developing a website, creating an app, starting a podcast, recording an audiobook of your book, etc.

Capture them all, even if you have to add birds to the sky and worms on the ground. Fill your whole orchard with ideas. You don't need to be precious about it, but if you want to make it pretty, feel free to play around with colored pencils, markers, or paints. Let's not reserve play for children; it's one of the best ways to connect with our creative selves.

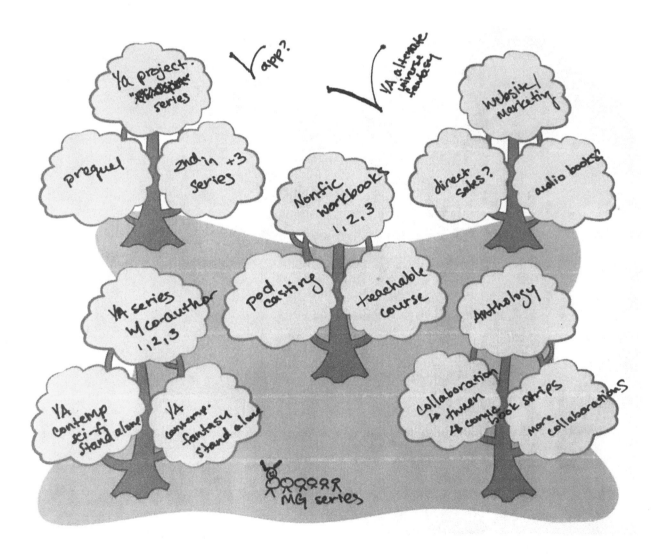

Worksheet 1: WIN AT CREATING YOUR IDEA ORCHARD

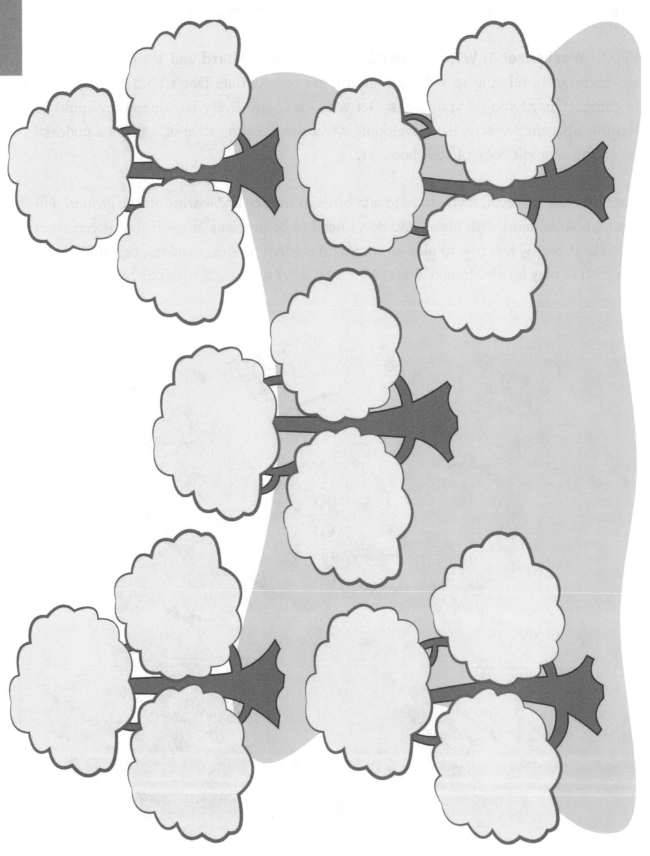

You'll have many ideas over the course of your creative life. Some you'll tend carefully and nurture into trees to produce fruit. Others you won't water or feed and they will be waiting in case you decide to tend to them. Being deliberate about where we put our time and energy is paramount.

Hopefully, you have an orchard full of ideas. If you only have one idea there, don't worry. Just keep adding to your orchard as creative ideas come to you. Your idea landscape and orchard are always changing.

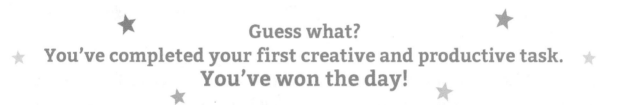

Guess what?
You've completed your first creative and productive task.
You've won the day!

Reward yourself! Play a quick game on your phone, scroll through social media, read a chapter of a book, or eat a piece of chocolate. Enjoy whatever small treat you want to give yourself.

When we experience small successes and reward ourselves for them, our brain gives us a rush of serotonin that makes us more likely to attack the next task. Every time you write, feeling great about it makes writing easier the next time!

Tip: Alongside my running TO-DO list that captures the errant thoughts that might interrupt my flow, I also keep a DONE list. I love the feeling I get when I write something down that I've completed! There's a DONE list you can use here when you check out of each day.

BONUS WIN: Want to dig deeper into creative play and productivity? Search for and watch Jane McGonigal's TED Talk *The Game That Can Give You Ten Extra Years of Life*.

BONUS WIN WIN: Incorporate some of Jane's strategies into your creative process. Come up with a kick-butt writing alter ego. Grab some allies. Identify tvvvvhe bad guys. Figure out your power-ups, or ways to feed your creativity so you come back to tomorrow with a stronger score on your creative excitement.

Author's Thank You Note: Thank you to author **Alicia Gregoire-Poirier** for always bringing the fun, whether we are brainstorming our ideas or our world-building. Or literally anything else we decide to do!

DONE LIST:

1. Brainstormed all our ideas into our Idea Orchard
2. _____
3. _____
4. _____
5. _____

RATE YOURSELF ON THE FOLLOWING SCALE.

Today's creative process flowed for me:

Not flowed **0 1 2 3 4 5 6 7 8 9 10** Totally flowed

Lastly, you can't WIN if you don't show up!
Commit to coming back to this workbook again.

MY PLAN FOR NEXT WRITING BLOCK:

You can't win if you don't show up! Make a commitment to come back to this workbook again. State the exact time and then make sure to keep the date.

Date: _____

Time: _____

Discover Your Mission

Day 2 Task: Pull out our crystal balls, look at the future, and brainstorm some more.

CHECK-IN:

I'm excited to create:

Not excited   **0 1 2 3 4 5 6 7 8 9 10**   Totally excited

I'm focused today:

Not focused   **0 1 2 3 4 5 6 7 8 9 10**   Totally focused

All right, let's do this! Remember yesterday's WIN?

We WIN our writing life by creating small successes every time we write. Sometimes when we're excited about making a change, we want to change everything all at once. If you've ever tried this, you've realized that a lot of change is hard to sustain. Instead, through this workbook, we're building momentum through small, sustainable, successes.

Now you have an Idea Orchard of possible projects. Keep an open mind and when you think of new projects you want to work on, update your Idea Orchard. Right now, while your ideas percolate, let's focus on the future!

TODAY'S FIRST ACTIVITY TO WIN: BRAINSTORM FIVE- AND ONE-YEAR GOALS

Overall vision: Let's project far enough into the future that you could imagine huge change. Where do you want to be, creatively, in five years? What projects do you want to have finished; what kind of fan base do you want? What skills do you want to learn?

You may be surprised to realize that these thoughts are rolling around in your mind. Getting them out helps us think about them, work with them, and realize them. Right now, we're just brainstorming. This means turn off your internal editor and just list everything that comes to mind. There are no wrong answers here!

When you brainstorm, think about everything you want to do that relates to your writing career. It might include submitting manuscripts at a conference, learning to write great dialogue, creating a website, writing ten short stories, etc.

Worksheet 2: WIN AT BRAINSTORMING THE FUTURE

Brainstorm writing-related projects you're thinking about doing in the next five years here.

Now, think in terms of the next 365 days. What writing-related projects do you want to take on sooner rather than later?

Next, we'll focus on our mission (statement).

TODAY'S SECOND ACTIVITY TO WIN: WRITE YOUR MISSION

Like an elevator pitch of a book, our mission statement describes, in a nutshell what we are doing and why.

For example, here's a mission statement I sometimes use as my bio: Heather Kelly explores the fabric of the universe through writing MG, YA, and everything in between. She wears many hats—teacher, editor, author, mentor, director. She's always searching for (and finding) ways to help authors become more prolific storytellers. Heather thrives on collaboration, creativeness, and community.

At the core of my mission statement is the idea of helping fellow authors, which incorporates my nonfiction and mentoring endeavors, and inquisitively looking at the possibilities (real or imagined) of the universe through writing MG, Tween, and YA novels.

Because I have two distinct missions—helping authors and writing books—I can break those two missions into two separate statements and career facets. When you look at your brainstormed tasks, you might be able to do the same.

Every task you work on in your writing life should feed your mission(s).

Worksheet 3: WIN AT YOUR MISSION

Brainstorm your mission(s) here. Write down everything that comes to mind about you and your writing:

Turn your mission into a statement that you can use as a bio or a statement that encapsulates your writing career.

_____

_____

_____

_____

_____

_____

_____

_____

_____

_____

Day 2

BONUS WIN: For an alternative creative business plan, consider going to Jane Friedman's website for authors where she posts Angela Ackerman's The 7-Step Business Plan for Writers. Both Jane Friedman and Angela Ackerman have many helpful tools for authors if you want to do a deeper dive now or later!

Author's Thank You Note: Thank you to author **Anna Staniszewski** for being one of the most hardworking people I know and pushing me to be the same. Thanks for always supporting my goals and holding me accountable to my missions!

DONE LIST:

1. Brainstormed five-year goals

2. Brainstormed one-year goals

3. Wrote a mission statement

4. _____

5. _____

★ ★

★ **Great job! You've won the day!** ★

★ ★

CHECK-OUT:

Today's creative process flowed for me:

Not flowed   **0 1 2 3 4 5 6 7 8 9 10**   Totally flowed

MY PLAN FOR NEXT WRITING BLOCK:

You can't win if you don't show up! Make a commitment to come back to this workbook again. State the exact time and then make sure to keep the date.

Date: _____

Time: _____

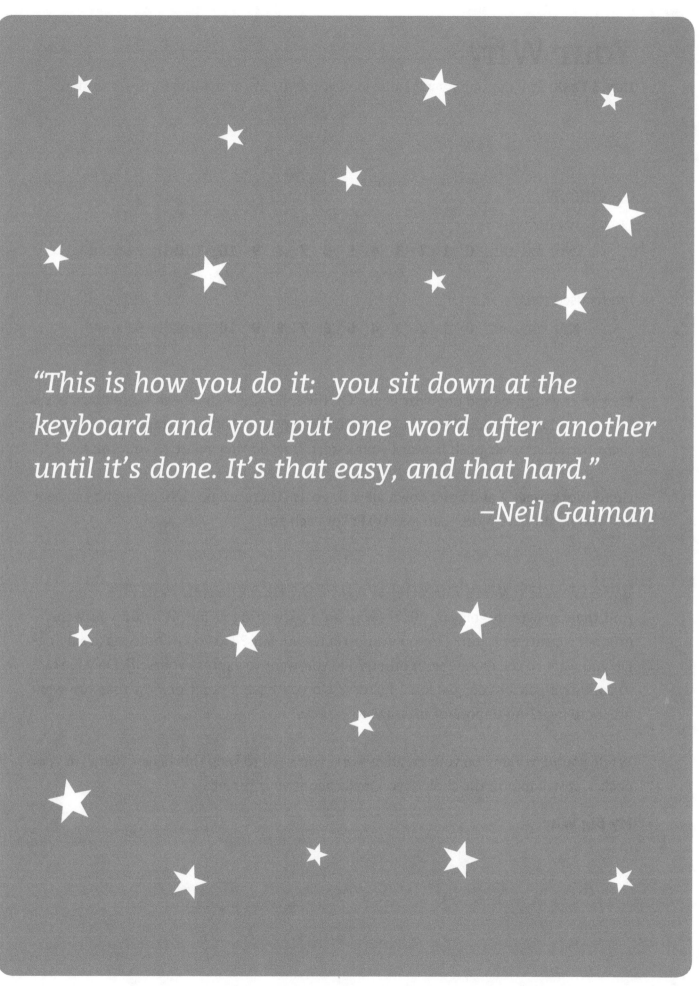

"This is how you do it: you sit down at the keyboard and you put one word after another until it's done. It's that easy, and that hard."

–Neil Gaiman

Your Why

Day 3 Task: Pull out our crystal balls, look at the future, and brainstorm some more.

CHECK-IN:

I'm excited to create:

Not excited **0 1 2 3 4 5 6 7 8 9 10** Totally excited

I'm focused today:

Not focused **0 1 2 3 4 5 6 7 8 9 10** Totally focused

Look over your five- and one-year goals. On the following worksheet, write down every answer to the question: WHY do you have these goals? And very importantly, how do these particular goals push forward your career; how do they relate to your mission?

Go to **Worksheet 4** and write down all your goals. There are no right or wrong answers, and you might have more than one **WHY** for each goal.

BIGGER WHY: WHY DO YOU WANT TO CREATE AND WRITE?

And then answer the bigger WHY—why are you writing at all? Why do you want to produce a creative project? Do you want to entertain fans? Do you want to make a living? Do you want to collaborate with others? Do you want to express yourself? Do you want to solidify a part of your personal history? Do you have a point of view that you want others to hear? An important message to express?

While you're working on your creative work, you need to keep this bigger "why" in your pocket. It will inform the choices you make about your career.

My Big Why:

Day
3

Goal: _____
_____

Why: _____
_____
_____

Goal: _____
_____

Why: _____
_____
_____

Goal: _____
_____

Why: _____
_____
_____

Goal: _____
_____

Why: _____
_____
_____

Goal: _____
_____

Why: _____
_____
_____

Goal: _____
_____

Why: _____
_____
_____

Goal: _____

_____

Why: _____

_____

_____

Goal: _____

_____

Why: _____

_____

_____

Goal: _____

_____

Why: _____

_____

_____

Goal: _____

_____

Why: _____

_____

_____

Goal: _____

_____

Why: _____

_____

_____

Goal: _____

_____

Why: _____

_____

_____

BONUS WIN: Check out the StoryShop podcast, Episode 02: *The Passion to Write*. Sean Platt, Johnny B. Truant, and David Wright talk about writing for different reasons: to share stories, for income, and more.

DONE LIST:

1. Brainstormed my goals and why I want to work on them.

2. Found my WHY!

3. _____

4. _____

⭐ ⭐ ⭐
Great job! You've won the day!
⭐ ⭐

CHECK-OUT:

Today's creative process flowed for me:

Not flowed **0 1 2 3 4 5 6 7 8 9 10** Totally flowed

MY PLAN FOR NEXT WRITING BLOCK:

You can't win if you don't show up! Make a commitment to come back to this workbook again. State the exact time and then make sure to keep the date.

Date: _____

Time: _____

Author's Thank You Note: Thank you to my writing partner, **Natasha Sass** for the amazing collaboration which feeds my WHY. And thanks to her for introducing me to Sean, Johnny, and David! Their ideas jumpstarted a fun time in my writing life, and if you dive deep into their podcasts, you might experience the same.

Say YES

Day 4 Tasks: Win at goal setting and saying yes. ☺

I'm excited to create:

Not excited **0 1 2 3 4 5 6 7 8 9 10** Totally excited

I'm focused today:

Not focused **0 1 2 3 4 5 6 7 8 9 10** Totally focused

So far, you've brainstormed your projects in an Idea Orchard, you've brainstormed your five- and one-year goals, and discovered your mission and your why. The best way to reach success is to know exactly what success looks like and the steps to get there. We need to break down our goals into doable, bite-sized, winnable pieces.

TODAY'S ACTIVITY TO WIN: BREAK GOALS INTO STEPS

Take another look at your brainstorming in your orchard and at the other worksheet s you've completed so far.

Your year's to-dos might be multifaceted. You may be working on several parts of your career at once—marketing through website building/maintenance, etc., producing products, and building your community. You may also focus on research and developing your craft.

Your long-term goals reflect what kind of writer you want to be, and what is important to you and your brand. We'll take a deeper dive into your brand on day twenty-four.

Goals you set for yourself are attainable and meaningful.

Attainable means that you must be able to cut the goal up into doable, daily to-dos. And that you can reach your goals without being dependent on things outside of your control. While you might want to make a million dollars on your writing or get an agent or publish traditionally, those are goals are dependent on the actions of other people.

Meaningful goals should relate to your **WHY** and mission statement. Your goals must be true to you. Not what you think you should do. Take the word "should" out of your vocabulary. Just because your critique partner wants to indie-publish a book doesn't mean that is the right path for you. Maybe you don't want to do all the production tasks that come along with indie-publishing. Or, just because all the other people in your critique group want to have their book traditionally published doesn't mean that you need to make a goal of researching agents or attending a conference that focuses on the traditional market. Maybe you have a creative vision for your book and want to retain creative control through indie publishing.

So, right now, list each one-year goal and the steps you need to take to complete those goals. Make these steps concrete. Here are some examples.

TO WRITE MORE EFFECTIVE DIALOGUE, YOUR STEPS MIGHT BE:

1. Read a craft book.
2. Take a workshop on dialogue.
3. Work with a critique group or mentor.

TO WRITE FIVE PICTURE BOOKS, YOUR STEPS MIGHT BE:

1. Find five mentor texts at the library and read.
2. Brainstorm topics.
3. Carve out an hour a day to write.
4. Run the manuscript by a critique group.
5. Revise.
6. Repeat for each manuscript.

TO FINISH A NOVEL, YOUR STEPS MIGHT BE:

1. Carve out an hour each day to write.
2. Write.
3. Send to crit partner.
4. Revise.

Worksheet 5: WIN AT BREAKING GOALS INTO DOABLE STEPS

Goal: _____

_____

Steps: _____

_____

_____

_____

_____

_____

_____

Goal: _____

_____

Steps: _____

_____

_____

_____

_____

_____

_____

Goal: _____

_____

Steps: _____

_____

_____

_____

_____

_____

_____

Tip: Need more room? Make copies of Worksheet Five from the Appendix.

Review your goals. Are they attainable? Meaningful? It's critical to keep experiencing success. We don't want to set ourselves up for failure; that's how people give up on their creative careers. Be gentle and kind to yourself and be **REASONABLE**. If you succeed at everything in your one-year plan in six months, you can add more goals!

The most important thing that keeps us working when the going gets tough is that we know WHY we are doing what we are doing.

Everyone has ideas. Many people say they want to write a book. The difference is that some people focus on an idea, work hard, learn what they need to know, work more, and bring the idea to fruition. That's what this workbook is about. But it's also about getting your creativity into shape. Nurturing yourself while you do the hard work, so that when you finish this idea and bring it to fruition, you are in an even better place to do it again.

Now that you know what your one-year goals are, pick a project from your Idea Orchard and goal setting page. Maybe the exercise from Section Three, thinking about why you want to do each goal, helped you narrow down the idea you want to pick first.

Take a moment and imagine this idea as a finished product. Some indie authors get their cover art at this stage because it's so inspiring to think of the book as a real, finished, thing!

When you have that visual in your head, come up with one or two lines that describe the gist of your project. The pitch. The main idea. The log line. How you would explain this project to anyone who didn't know what you were working on. Fill in Worksheet Six and use it as your cheat-sheet going forward!

Worksheet 6: WIN AT SAYING YES!

Name of my product:

_____

_____

One sentence about my product (a pitch):

_____

_____

_____

_____

_____

Why I want to create this product right now:

_____

_____

_____

_____

_____

_____

My goal for completion of this project (time frame):

_____

_____

The steps I'm taking to complete this project:

1. _____   6. _____

   _____   _____

2. _____   7. _____

   _____   _____

3. _____   8. _____

   _____   _____

4. _____   9. _____

   _____   _____

5. _____   10. _____

   _____   _____

Understanding our goals and our WHY for writing helps us say YES to things that line up with our values. Knowing when to say YES is one of the most important things we'll think about on this journey. When we say YES to things that feed us, things that bring us closer to our goal, and when we are open to opportunities that line up with our values, our careers and lives change in ways we couldn't have predicted.

If you excel at getting things done and want to work on two projects at the same time, use a second **Workshop 6** from the Appendix to get you on track.

BONUS WIN: Check out Kwame Alexander's TED Talk *The Power of YES*. He will fire you up to be open to all opportunities!

Author's Thank You Note: Thank you to **Kwame Alexander** for saying 'Yes' when I asked him to give an impromptu keynote presentation at the NE-SCBWI conference when he thought he was just giving a workshop!

DONE LIST:

1. _____

2. _____

3. _____

★ **You've won the day!** ★
★ **You've said YES to a project and broke it down into parts!** ★
★ ★

CHECK-OUT:

Today's creative process flowed for me:

Not flowed **0 1 2 3 4 5 6 7 8 9 10** Totally flowed

MY PLAN FOR NEXT WRITING BLOCK:

Date: _____

Time: _____

Day 5

Your WHY NOT and Finding Gratitude

Day 5 Tasks: Examine your demons. And take them down. And then get all zen.

CHECK-IN:

I'm excited to create:

Not excited   **0 1 2 3 4 5 6 7 8 9 10**   Totally excited

I'm focused today:

Not focused   **0 1 2 3 4 5 6 7 8 9 10**   Totally focused

Every time we take the risk to create something, we pull along our deepest fears. Creating feels very personal. It's an extension of the inner self. It can make us feel vulnerable. So, let's face those fears together.

TODAY'S FIRST ACTIVITY TO WIN: BRAINSTORM FEARS

Take the next minute (yes, time yourself) and brainstorm the fears that block you from working on your chosen project and creating enthusiastically.

Fears:

Great. Now take one more minute and write down fears you avoided during that first minute. The deep dark ones that keep you from your goals and success.

Deeper Fears:

My fears are pretty typical: Maybe I'm not good enough. Maybe my writing isn't good enough. Fear of failure—and success. But knowing those fears, I can weigh my options. I can decide not to risk letting others see my creative projects and not grow as a creative person, or I can find the support in other people and take the risks to get my stuff out there. I'm a big fan of surrounding myself with people who won't let me fail.

The bottom line is, right now, you are enough. I'm here to tell you that wherever you are on your writing journey at the moment is the perfect place to be.

And the more you are comfortable with creating, the more you will grow as a creator, and be able to express yourself on paper the way you want to.

Remember, fear is universal and necessary. Creating without fear isn't authentic. Embrace your authentic self and create alongside the fear.

These fears may be the irritants that roll around your brain when you try to create: "This book sucks." "I'll never be good at writing." "I'm not a real writer."

By naming your fears, you've taken away some of their power. When we take things and look at them in the light, they don't seem as potent.

We get better at what we practice. If we let these voices rattle around our mind when we try to create, we get better at fearing, not at creating.

WE CAN USE EVIDENCE TO UNDERMINE OUR FEARS:

Fear: I'm not good at writing, so why am I trying it?
Evidence: (against it) When I show people my writing, they like it or at least some aspects of it. Of course, it needs work, but I'm a hard worker. I'm willing to put the effort in.

Fear: I don't know enough to write this manuscript.
Evidence: I love to learn, and will research what I need to in order to make this manuscript strong.

Fear: No one will ever read my writing.
Evidence: I know writers who would read my story if I asked them to.

Sometimes we need to combat our fears, or "why nots," with our "whys."

Fear: This project will never be good enough.
But: I'm not writing this project to please others; I'm writing it to please myself. And I'm pretty discerning. And I have supporters who can help me make my work better. Nobody, including myself, will let me put something out in the world that isn't worthy.

Fear: I don't have enough time to finish a project.
But: I love creating and it feeds me, which is why I'm doing this. Even if it takes a long time, I will still be fed by working on this creative project.

Fear: People will give my book bad reviews.
But: Not everyone will like my book, and that's okay. I'm not writing for everyone.

Now, use the following worksheet to combat your fears!

Worksheet 7: WIN AT DEFEATING FEARS

Fear: _____

_____

Evidence or But: _____

_____

Fear: _____

_____

Evidence or But: _____

_____

Fear: _____

_____

Evidence or But: _____

_____

Fear: _____

_____

Evidence or But: _____

_____

Fear: _____

_____

Evidence or But: _____

_____

Fear: _____

_____

Evidence or But: _____

_____

Keep going until you combat every fear. Pay attention to the thoughts in your head and stop the fears in their tracks. Be ready with evidence or your WHYs to take down those fears. If you need a second worksheet, find it in the Appendix.

ACTIVITY TWO TO WIN TODAY: DEVELOP TOOLS OF GRATITUDE AND FORGIVENESS

We've spent a lot of time with our fears, and now I want to take a few minutes to focus on developing some of the best tools to combat doubt and anxiety: gratitude and forgiveness.

Some writers use daily affirmations. Why? Because it changes the way our brain chemistry works. Practicing gratitude for what we have and forgiveness for the mistakes we make changes our brain chemistry in the same way.

Writing is hard. Every day is different, and many days are solitary. We can have critique partners and cheerleaders, but we have to do the hard work ourselves.

Most writers deal with shades of doubt at some point—from facing rejections, seeing others' successes, feeling stuck, or the difficulty of creating, among other things. Even just from living in our heads too long while creating our stories.

You can protect yourself from these feelings by practicing gratitude and forgiveness.

Before you start your writing day (or just your day!) make a list of things that you are grateful for.

Today, I'm grateful for the time I have to work on my writing, plus my family, my friends, and my determination.

Easy, right?

And let's forgive ourselves for our mistakes.

Today, I forgive myself for not being as far along as I wanted to be in my writing project. I forgive myself for speaking before thinking yesterday and for overbooking myself today.

Worksheet 8: WIN AT DEFEATING FEARS

Make a list here of some of the things you are grateful for today:

_____

_____

_____

_____

_____

_____

_____

_____

_____

_____

What do you forgive yourself for?

_____

_____

_____

_____

_____

_____

_____

_____

_____

_____

_____

When we let go of the self-deprecating thoughts and forgive ourselves, and then remind ourselves of what we have, we set the stage for optimum work. Some people say to turn off the inner editor. I say, let go of the mistakes of the past, and remind ourselves of what we can be thankful for. This clears the cache, as it is, of negative thoughts that roll around our heads, and instead fill our heads with a positive reality.

If you deal with anxiety or depression, find someone to talk to! Just as it's easier to write with someone else (i.e., this manual), some problems can't be solved alone.

In her book, My Stroke of Insight, neuroscientist Jill Bolte Taylor notes that emotions only live for 90 seconds. Any time you feel the physiological effects of your emotions for longer than that, it is because you're feeding them. We get better at what we practice. Practice feeding positive emotions by replacing negative self-talk with gratitude and forgiveness.

BONUS WIN: Search for the TED Talk *Plug Into Your Hard-Wired Happiness* with Srikumar Rao, where he talks convincingly about focusing not on the outcome but investing in the journey.

BONUS BONUS WIN: It's all about perspective. Watch the TED Talk with Matthew Dicks *Live Life Like You Are 100-Years Old*. I had the fortunate experience of being present when he gave this talk. It's got a lot of tough stuff in it but it's amazing. You can take a deeper dive with Matthew Dicks into his other TED Talk, *Homework for Life*, which is particularly useful to writers and those moments that are the kernels of truth that allow writers to connect emotionally with readers! Check it out for an extra bonus WIN today! And if you are looking for story ideas to add to your Idea Garden, definitely do Matthew Dicks' homework!

I'm asking you to consider a lot. Remember that we aren't trying to change everything right now. Small successes matter. You may want to come back and do deeper dives after you finish this workbook, to continue winning!

DONE LIST:

1. _____

2. _____

3. _____

CHECK-OUT:

Today's creative process flowed for me:

Not flowed **0 1 2 3 4 5 6 7 8 9 10** Totally flowed

MY PLAN FOR NEXT WRITING BLOCK:

Date: _____

Time: _____

Author's Thank You Note: I'm most grateful for **Scott, David, Sean,** and **Caitlin** and for the love and support they give me day in and day out. In a hundred years I will look back and know that while writing fed me, my time spent with all of you was most important!

We Get Better at What We Practice

Day 6 Task: Frame out the actual work.

CHECK-IN:

I'm excited to create:

Not excited   **0 1 2 3 4 5 6 7 8 9 10**   Totally excited

I'm focused today:

Not focused   **0 1 2 3 4 5 6 7 8 9 10**   Totally focused

My Writing WHY: _____

Today, I'm grateful for: _____

Today, I forgive myself for: _____

We've talked about our fears. What happens when we practice fearful thoughts? We get better at ... fearful thinking. When we practice gratitude and forgiveness, we get better at grace.

When we practice writing, we get better at WRITING!

When you sit down to write, what do you do? Do you go on social media? Do you check your email? Do you get right to work in your manuscript?

Be mindful of your habits. When you think you've spent a good amount of time writing, but you've actually been surfing the web, you've been practicing distraction and procrastination. Another phenomenon to note is that when we talk with other people about our writing, it tricks our brain into thinking that we are creating. So, we don't want to practice talking about writing instead of practice writing.

Practice positive self-talk. Practice good creating. Practice writing through the fear. Practice saying yes to the journey. We get better at what we practice.

Remember to forgive yourself for past mistakes and to be grateful for what you have.

Half the battle of practicing writing is knowing exactly what we are going to do next. Before you end a writing session, write down the next day's to-do list for writing. I've added a space for you to do this in your check-out.

TODAY'S FIRST ACTIVITY TO WIN: CREATE YOUR TO-DO LIST

Let's dive deep into what you'll need to practice in order to create your project.
On the following worksheet, write down what you need to do or to take on, in order to get this project done. Take the work you did on Worksheet Six and break the steps into daily to-dos.

Every to-do on your list should be small enough to complete in one writing session. If you're writing a novel, your to-do items may include: write 1,000 words, write a killer opening line for chapter one, etc. If you're revising a manuscript, you may include to-dos like: Read chapter one like a reader and highlight changes to make, or send fifty pages to my critique group, etc.

Write down every small to-do in order to get this project done!

Worksheet 9: WIN AT TO-DO LISTING

Name of my project: _____

_____

List of to-dos:

Creatively WIN   Jumpstart Your Writing in Thirty Days   heatherkellyauthor.com

ACTIVITY TWO TO WIN TODAY: PLEDGING AND RAMPING UP

When you train for a marathon, you don't run 26.2 miles on the first day. Maybe aim for a mile. (Or half a mile!)

The whole idea behind this jumpstart of your writing is that you experience success. Every. Single. Day. That you get a win each time you sit down to write.

Think about that for a moment. Our goal is not just to get our writing goals accomplished, but to set the stage to accomplish our writing goals in the future. And we do that by creating a habit and nurturing our creativity.

Right now, pledge that you will sit down to write every time that you intend to. Your ideal schedule might be once a week, or every weekday, but it must fit into your life. And it must acknowledge the ebbs and flows in our lives. Summer schedules are sometimes different from fall schedules. Holiday schedules are different from non-holiday schedules.

When you have an ideal schedule in mind, be flexible. Maybe you want to write every single day for an hour. Maybe you want to write Monday through Friday for two hours. Maybe you want to write on the weekends when you're not tired from your day job.

So, what is your ideal goal? It may be a time goal that fits into your current life schedule or a word count goal. I like a time goal because I know I can hit as long as I work during that time. I don't always know I'll hit a word-count goal, even if I work hard. Word-count goals are fun during NaNoWriMo (National Novel Writing Month), though! Be detailed with your ideal goal. If you know that you have less time, schedule less writing on that day. Be specific and make the goal attainable.

My pledge for my writing schedule is: _____

_____

Block out your writing schedule on your calendar.
These are writing sessions that, barring a crisis, you will keep.

Now, let's talk about ramping up our to-do list. If you've listed to-dos that include writing 1,000 words a day, every day, then for the first week, reduce that to-do item down to 250 words a day. It may feel small, but you will hit that goal. Those successes will make you feel better about writing and you will be more likely to get your "butt in chair" on the next day. The second week, up your writing to 500 words. Then 750.

By week four, you will be hitting your ideal writing to-do for the day, or you won't. And if you aren't, be flexible. Did you feel confident at 500 words a day? 750? Back down your ideal goal to whatever pace made you feel great about writing and ready to attack it the next day.

If your ideal writing to-do is to write an hour a day, or spend one hour on writing and one hour on marketing or whatnot, then start the first week with 15 minutes. If that feels comfortable the first day, continue that amount for that week. Then the second week bump it up to 30, the third, 45 minutes, the fourth, an hour.

Tip: The Pomodoro Technique is effective for getting yourself into the writing zone. It's a method of focusing for a certain amount of time on a task and then taking a small break, utilizing timers to bring you into your work and out. Check it out online (search for Pomodoro Technique).

Tip: A lot of writers jumpstart their writing with NaNoWriMo, when writers pledge to write 50,000 words during the month of November. It's a month full of excitement and writing fever, and I love it! If you're up for it and have done the pre-work necessary to write a novel, go for it. However, a lot of writers can't sustain the 1,667 drafting words for the entire year. Many writers feel burned out after the month. We're aiming here for high productivity and low burn-out! Every writer is different; the point is to know yourself and your abilities.

The optimal way to sustain your writing goals is to experience repeated successes with flexibility. You're probably not going to write on a major holiday, or when you are on vacation with the in-laws. That's bonus time. Don't expect to work on your writing during those days—and if you get a chance to write, it's an unexpected gift to yourself.

Small successes are the best way to achieve big successes.

So, with your writing schedule in front of you, go back to your list of to-dos on Worksheet Nine, and add a date to accomplish each one. Make sure you've adjusted the first few to-dos so that you are ramping up and not running a writing marathon on day one! Then plug each to-do into your calendar. Aim to honor your writing pledge. When you respect yourself and your time you can accomplish anything!

It's important to put ourselves first and practice creativity. When we pay into our creative work and treat that as important, then our creativity starts to become nourished and we feel more fulfilled.

Great job! You've won the day!
Reward yourself and look forward to coming back to start knocking off those writing to-dos!

BONUS WIN: Become an active participant in your decisions for writing! Check out the TED Talk *How to Achieve Your Most Ambitious Goals* with Stephen Duneier. You could see amazing results by taking big assignments and breaking them down into the simplest tasks and making marginal adjustments to your daily routines!

DONE LIST:

1. _____

2. _____

3. _____

CHECK-OUT:

Today's creative process flowed for me:

Not flowed **0 1 2 3 4 5 6 7 8 9 10** Totally flowed

Review your writing plans for tomorrow and get psyched for **day One of writing!**

MY PLAN FOR NEXT WRITING BLOCK:

Date: _____

Time: _____

TO-DOS I WILL ACCOMPLISH:

_____   _____

_____   _____

_____   _____

_____   _____

_____   _____

First Day of Writing and Stocking Your Toolbox

Day 7 Tasks: Open up our toolboxes, stock them with all sorts of goodies, and start writing.

CHECK-IN:

I'm excited to create:

Not excited **0 1 2 3 4 5 6 7 8 9 10** Totally excited

I'm focused today:

Not focused **0 1 2 3 4 5 6 7 8 9 10** Totally focused

My Writing WHY: _____

Today, I'm grateful for: _____

Today, I forgive myself for: _____

Go and work on the project you chose to focus on; we'll wait for you.

When you're done, write it into your Done List at the end of this section. Make notes for what to-dos you will work on during your next writing session. Reward yourself! You've won the day!

Tip: I love streaks. Doing things each day for a stretch of days. And I hate breaking a streak. If I keep track of my streaks, it motivates me to write or exercise on a day I'm feeling tired! There are apps that can do this for you, or you can just keep track of your streaks on a calendar. Don't break the streaks!

TODAY'S ACTIVITY TO WIN: FIND YOUR TOOLS

Now, let's chat a bit about what to do when the going gets tough.

There are lots of times when writing can get tough. When those pesky negative thoughts start rolling around our head and we're not quick enough at banishing them. Or maybe other things in life other than writing pull you down. And then there's the vulnerability.

When we start writing for fans, we make ourselves vulnerable. Right now, you may be drafting, which I always think is telling ourselves our story. When we revise, we start the process of telling our story to someone else. After revising, you'll probably run your story by critiquers. And maybe send it off in query to an agent. Or, if you're an indie publisher, you'll hire an editor and start the process of putting together your package.

> **However you plan on getting that story out, you're going to show it to others—you know, just, the world.**

Critiques can be hard to receive. Even when it's positive, a critique means that the hard work isn't finished. And you will continue to face rejection when you show your work to others: negative reviews, agents and editors who say "no."

So, today, we'll focus on what we store in our emotional toolbox—items that we pull out when we recognize that our emotional reserve is low and needs a boost. It's one of the reasons we start each day in this workbook with a check-in. We need to take a look at our emotional thermometer. And then use the tools to raise our emotional thermometer to within the range of optimally, creatively working.

Take a look at Worksheet Ten on the following page and highlight any of the tools there that you would be interested in trying out when you feel down and don't want to write. When you are dealing with rejection or when you don't know what to do next.

Add tools that you use when the going gets tough to boost your emotional thermometer.

Author's Thank You Note: Thank you to **Kristen Wixted** for always being a tool In my toolbox, I mean! Whenever I need inspiration, validation, or excitement for a project, I know you are only a phone call away. Thanks for injecting my toolbox with humor and a kick in the pants.

Worksheet 10: WIN AT BUILDING A TOOLBOX OF BIG TOOLS

- Journaling
- Exercising/working out/being on a sports team
- Joining an advocacy group or religious center
- Reading/listening to an audio book
- Socializing
- Watching TV/a movie
- Talking to a friend/family member
- Caring for a pet
- Being creative in other ways: drawing, photography, knitting, baking
- Creating a list of to-dos and getting them done
- Singing/playing musical instruments
- Walking

- Playing a game with others or alone
- Being outside
- Talking with a therapist/religious official
- Going to group therapy
- Going to the chiropractor/masseuse
- Going shopping
- Watching TED Talks
- Cooking
- Volunteering
- Meditating
- Going away on vacation!
- Listening to music
- Dancing
- Listening to a podcast

Others tools that aren't on the list that you want to use when the going gets tough:

_____   _____

_____   _____

_____   _____

_____   _____

Now, list your top five tools that resonate with you.

Top Five Big Tools:

1. _____
2. _____
3. _____
4. _____
5. _____

When you prep for your writing time, check in with yourself, and find that your emotional well needs a boost for you to feel ready to create, now you have a plan for what to do.

You might have noticed a pattern here. We have a plan for our career; for what we're doing over the next year and the next five years. We developed a plan with daily steps for the creative project we've chosen to work on. Every day we set the plan for tomorrow. And now we have a plan for what happens when our emotions are depleted and we need to refill the well in order to do our creative work.

Knowing what step is next every day is the best way to keep our momentum going on our creative project. There is no guesswork. We don't have to stop mid-project and figure out what's next. We always know what's next.

And we get it done!

So, those are the big tools we use when we are feeling emotionally down about working forward.

But sometimes when we're in the middle of our writing, we experience frustration. Mostly we stop writing when we 1. don't know how to do the next thing, 2. know something needs to change, but don't know how yet, or 3. we doubt ourselves and our writing.

The tools that we need for these times when we stop writing during our planned writing time because we are frustrated need to be smaller tools. Tools that we can pull out, use in a small amount of time, and then jump back into our writing.

These tools can be thought of as beneficial distractions that change the brain loop that is telling us that we can't do what comes next, don't know how to do what comes next, or shouldn't do what comes next.

These distractions give the brain time to stop the negative loop it's experiencing and figure out how to solve the writing puzzle we have in front of us.

Worksheet 11:
WIN AT BUILDING YOUR TOOLBOX of IN–THE MOMENT (small) TOOLS

- Reaching out to a writing partner
- Playing a five-minute game on your phone/computer/tablet
- Taking a brief walk
- Watching a short video
- Listening to music
- Getting a drink
- Zoning out for ten minutes
- Visualizing your product finished
- Eating—because maybe your brain is hungry!
- Listening to a short podcast
- Brainstorming what comes next

Add your own tools here:

1. _____
2. _____
3. _____
4. _____
5. _____

Now, list your top five tools that resonate with you.

Top Five Small Tools:

1. _____
2. _____
3. _____
4. _____
5. _____

These tools are quick, change your brain chemistry, and get you right back into writing.

Note when you want to step away from writing, what the hard things are for you. Have a plan in place for those times so you can take a break from writing and then get right back into it.

It's also important that you don't choose an activity that is a rabbit hole for you—an activity that leads to another that leads to another. One positive tool for one person can be a rabbit hole that derails someone else's writing time. Know yourself and what works for you!

Tip: I like to use timers to make sure that I'm spending the time I want on my writing! When I'm in the zone I will reset the timer (for me, a timing cube) as needed. But when writing is a struggle, I will use the cube as a way to stay on track by small chunks of time I intend to work.

Let's take your favorite tools from Worksheets Ten and Eleven and build your best toolbox. Choose the top five big tools for when you are emotionally depleted and the top five in-the-moment tools for when you are feeling frustrated in the middle of writing and add them to Worksheet Twelve.

Worksheet 12: WIN AT STOCKING TOOLBOXES

My Big Toolbox to Fill My Emotional Well:

1. _____
2. _____
3. _____
4. _____
5. _____

My Small Toolbox to Use in the Moment:

1. _____
2. _____
3. _____
4. _____
5. _____

Now, when you prep for your writing time, and check in with yourself, and find that your emotional well needs a boost for you to feel ready to create, you have a plan for what to do.

If you find that there is a day when you planned to get work done but didn't, read the section When You've Missed A Day, and afterward, come back to the section you were on before.

BONUS WIN: Check out how Josh Kaufman dispels the 10,000-hour rule in his TED Talk, *The First Twenty Hours: How to Learn Anything!*

DONE LIST:

1. Brainstormed best tools
2. Stocked your toolboxes
3. _____
4. _____

CHECK-OUT:

Today's creative process flowed for me:

Not flowed   **0 1 2 3 4 5 6 7 8 9 10**   Totally flowed

Review your writing plans for tomorrow
and get psyched for **day two of writing!**

MY PLAN FOR NEXT WRITING BLOCK:

Date: _____

Time: _____

TO-DOS I WILL ACCOMPLISH:

1. _____   3. _____
2. _____   4. _____

TOOLS I PLAN TO USE IF I BECOME FRUSTRATED:

1. _____   3. _____
2. _____   4. _____

Second Day of Writing and Knowing Your Strategies

Day 8 Tasks: Second day of writing and figure out strategies! Woo-hoo!

CHECK-IN:

I'm excited to create:

       Not excited **0 1 2 3 4 5 6 7 8 9 10** Totally excited

I'm focused today:

       Not focused **0 1 2 3 4 5 6 7 8 9 10** Totally focused

My Writing WHY: _____

Today, I'm grateful for: _____

Today, I forgive myself for: _____

So, first, write. You should have given yourself an achievable amount of work to do today. Small successes are the key!

Don't worry, I'll wait.

Are you back? Done with today's goal?

★   ★

★   **You've WON the Day! Reward yourself ! You did it!** ★

★   ★

Write it into your Done List at the bottom of the page and plan for your next writing session!

TODAY'S ACTIVITY TO WIN: OPTIMIZE STRATEGIES

As writers, it's compelling to compare what we do and our process with other writers, particularly if you're lucky enough to have a local writing community.

We hear the stories. The writer who writes a 60,000-word first draft and then deletes the entire first draft and starts over, claiming, it's always better the second time around.

(It is always better the second time around, but I will NEVER delete my first draft!) The writer who sits down in the morning (and doesn't drink coffee or tea) and doesn't move from their chair until they have five pages of work done. The writer who edits as they go so their first draft is a clean, revised draft. The writer who doesn't outline a word and then writes an entire book by the seat of their pants. The writer who writes a 20,000-word outline before starting and knows every last detail of every character and plot point before drafting a word of their novel.

Writers love to exchange how-tos. Write faster. Write cleaner. Write backwards.

The good news? Every. Single. Writer. Is. Different.
The bad news? Every. Single. Writer. Is. Different.

This means we get to discover how we best write. This means there is no one right way to write. We have to come up with our own strategies. And many authors will say they need a new strategy for every book. I do believe that most manuscripts will require a different revision tool than the ones before. A timeline. A map. Each manuscript may have a different challenge for its author.

Most likely, you already have some basics of how you work best, or strategies that help you construct your creative work. It's important to recognize and keep what works for you, and change what doesn't.

Maybe you:
• take a walk or run and think about the next scene you're going to write.
• see every scene play in your head before you write it.
• outline a sentence of each scene for the whole book before you start drafting.
• storyboard.
• world-build.

The best advice I've heard from an author is:
We draft to our strengths and revise to our weaknesses.

Think about your strengths. Knowing these will inform how you draft. If your strength is world building really dig in by building a file of pictures and descriptions of the world. Maybe you love character development and start by writing origin stories and flaws of your main characters before you draft. If your strengths are organization and plotting, then you may want to start looking at story beats for the genre you are writing in and outlining the plots along those beats.

By feeding your strengths you feed your creativity and make the process more fun. Besides thinking about your strengths, also think about what writing strategies work for you. Record these strengths and strategies on the next worksheet.

Some possible writing strategies you may want to try:

- Listening to a soundtrack specific to each project

- Writing in the same place every day

- Writing at the same time every day

- Exercising before each writing session

- Leaving your house to write

- Using timers or phones to keep track of writing blocks

- Writing in your pajamas so your internal editor stays away

- Getting dressed so you feel that your writing is a professional endeavor

- Writing before you check your email or do social media

Worksheet 13: WIN AT STRATEGIES

My writing strengths:

_____

_____

_____

_____

What time of day do I do my best writing?

_____

What type of environment do I like to create in?

_____

_____

How long do I like to work before taking a break?

_____

_____

If interrupted, can I go back to work?

_____

What other strategies work?

_____

_____

_____

What strategies would I like to try to optimize my writing sessions?

_____

_____

_____

_____

Day 8

It's important that you develop a workable creative flow, tailored to you. Review today's writing work. Did you use a strategy that works for you? Or did you try something new? Both are totally legit—sometimes we need to try something to see if it works.

During the thirty days you're working on this workbook, you may decide to try out different strategies to see if they make it easier to get into writing or easier to stay in the writing zone.

BONUS WIN: Search for the YouTube videos done by author Kate Cavanaugh, where she tries structuring her writing day like a famous author. Watch her mimic the writing strategies of authors like J. K. Rowling, Stephen King, Nora Roberts, and more! Remember, your goal is to figure out what works best for you. When Kate goes on this journey, she picks up tips and tricks that work for her and dismisses the patterns that don't.

**You don't need to write like anyone except yourself.
But taking a look at others' habits could help you
find something that works for you.**

Author's Thank You Note: Thank you to **Dave Pasquantonio** for always keeping me accountable, organized, and up-to-date with the latest writing gadgets. For starting great Loft groups that always turn out to be just what I need!

DONE LIST:

1. _____

2. _____

3. _____

4. _____

CHECK-OUT:

Today's creative process flowed for me:

Not flowed   **0   1   2   3   4   5   6   7   8   9   10**   Totally flowed

**Review your writing plans for tomorrow
and get psyched for day three of writing!**

MY PLAN FOR NEXT WRITING BLOCK:

Date: _____

Time: _____

TO-DOS I WILL ACCOMPLISH:

1. _____   3. _____

2. _____   4. _____

TOOLS I PLAN TO USE IF I BECOME FRUSTRATED:

1. _____   3. _____

2. _____   4. _____

Third Day of Writing and Workflow

Day 9 Tasks: Third day of writing and organize your writing life.

CHECK-IN:

I'm excited to create:

Not excited **0 1 2 3 4 5 6 7 8 9 10** Totally excited

I'm focused today:

Not focused **0 1 2 3 4 5 6 7 8 9 10** Totally focused

My Writing WHY: _____

Today, I'm grateful for: _____

Today, I forgive myself for: _____

First, like yesterday, do your ramp-up creative work. I'll wait for you to get that done.

Did you hit your writing goal? ⭐ **YES. Go you! You've WON the Day!** ⭐

Write that on your Done List, plan for the next writing session, and celebrate.

TODAY'S ACTIVITY TO WIN: ORGANIZE YOUR WORKFLOW

Now we're looking at your workflow. Where do you keep your manuscripts, ideas, and outlines, so that you can quickly enter your writing?

When you have a brilliant idea or snippet of dialogue, and you're away from your computer, how do you record it so you can later pop it into your manuscripts?

Workflow is important.

Workflow is important because of the FLOW. It's important to be organized, and have tools at your fingertips, so there is little transition between thought and work. Delay in getting into your manuscript creates a barrier between yourself and your creative process. Delay allows fears to creep back in.

If you have a solid organizational process, and great writing tools, and your workflow works well, list it on Worksheet Fourteen.

Worksheet 14: WIN AT WORKFLOW

I keep my ideas and notes here:

_____

_____

I keep my outlines here:

_____

_____

I keep my "book bible" (worldbuilding, story notes, etc.) here:

_____

_____

I write my manuscripts using this program:

_____

_____

I keep backups of my manuscripts here:

_____

_____

I keep lists of projects here:

_____

_____

I keep to-do lists and schedules here:

_____

_____

When I send manuscripts for critiques or edits, I name them this way:

_____

_____

Tools and craft guides I keep by my computer in case I need to use them:

_____

_____

Anything else I want to remember about my workflow:

_____

_____

If you don't have systems in place or something that works for you yet, decide how you can organize your writing flow so that you have what you need at your fingertips and you have little transition when you sit down to write.

A good rule of thumb for naming manuscripts is to use a date and the project name in the title. When you send a manuscript to someone else, include their last name, and the date, and the name of your project in the title. That way, if you're searching in Word or Scrivener for a project title, you know which version you sent to someone and which one is the most recent.

When you make significant changes to a manuscript, back it up. You can back up to an external drive, or to internet-based storage like drop-box, or you can email yourself your manuscript. Or do all of the above. No one method is fail-safe, and you don't want to lose your creative work.

Thinking about workflow reminds us that we are treating our writing life as importantly as we treat a business or profession. If we are going to put this much time and effort in, it's not a hobby.

BONUS WIN: Check out the videos of writer/educator/entrepreneur Nir Eyal, who helps us put technology in its place, and has it work for us instead of the other way around.

Tip: Consider implementing Nir Eyal's practice of helping technology give you traction instead of distraction. Set an alarm on your phone or device for when you want to begin your next writing work block.

BONUS BONUS WIN: Listen to The Creative Penn podcast in which author entrepreneur Joanna Penn interviews Nir Eyal. It's called How to Focus and Be Indistractable. Both experts, **Joanna Penn** and **Nir Eyal**, have excellent research and informative thinking to share.

Author's Thank You Note: Thank you to author **Lisa Papademetriou** for designing an amazing cloud-based tool called BookFlow, which has streamlined my writing process immensely! It saves me a ton of time since I can write and store all my writing-related things in one place online.

DONE LIST:

1. _____
2. _____
3. _____

CHECK-OUT:

Today's creative process flowed for me:

Not flowed   **0 1 2 3 4 5 6 7 8 9 10**   Totally flowed

Review your writing plans for tomorrow
and get psyched for **day four of writing!**

MY PLAN FOR NEXT WRITING BLOCK:

Date: _____

Time: _____

TO-DOS I WILL ACCOMPLISH:

1. _____   3. _____
2. _____   4. _____

TOOLS I PLAN TO USE IF I BECOME FRUSTRATED:

1. _____   3. _____
2. _____   4. _____

Fourth Day of Writing and Focusing on Fans

Day 10 Tasks: Day four of writing and think about who will enjoy our final product.

CHECK-IN:

I'm excited to create:

Not excited **0 1 2 3 4 5 6 7 8 9 10** Totally excited

I'm focused today:

Not focused **0 1 2 3 4 5 6 7 8 9 10** Totally focused

My Writing WHY: _____

Today, I'm grateful for: _____

Today, I forgive myself for: _____

Go ahead and write. When you're done, come back after you note today's session in your Done List! And plan for the next writing session.

Congrats at staying with your creative work for four days. Congrats at continuing to want to work at making your creative life stronger. Celebrate your successes! Go for a walk. Read a picture book or chapter of a book. Make tea. Do something you love to reward yourself.

★ **You've WON the Day!** ★

★ **As you carve out more time to write, the activities in this workbook** ★ **will be less lengthy. Focus more of your time on your creating!** ★

TODAY'S ACTIVITY TO WIN: FOCUS ON FANS

Remember that video of the first follower? That mass of people who follow you, starting with that first person, are your fans. You're writing to them. You want to write a satisfying story that is loved by your fans.

If you try to appeal to everyone, you will appeal to no one.

So, take a moment and describe your fan. This will inform what flag posts you will hit as you write. Are you writing to parents and kids reading books at bedtime? Are you writing to the YA and crossover adult fanbase? Are you writing to mystery fans?

Ideal fan: _____

_____

_____

_____

_____

_____

Knowing who your fan is, and having this person in mind as you draft, revise, and polish, will help you write. It will also help you when you're done with your book and you're thinking about marketing. Where do you find your fan? What type of book does your fan normally read? In what format: Ebooks? Paper books? Are they on social media? Would you interact with them?

Once you know who your fan is, you can figure out what your mentor texts will be. What other books does your fan enjoy? Read those books for understanding of when you need to hit your guideposts, and what those guideposts might be. See what books your fan is reading, by checking which books are the top sellers at big online book retailers. You want your book to fit alongside those books, and be a satisfying read for those fans.

List possible mentor texts (books that are similar to your work-in-progress that you will share fans with; books your book will sit next to at the bookstore):

_____

_____

_____

_____

_____

_____

_____

BONUS WIN: Go to the library or bookstore and get some of your mentor texts so you can see what your fans like to read. Pay attention to the blurb on the back of the book and think about how your pitch compares.

BONUS BONUS WIN: If your writing project is a novel or screenplay, Check out Blake Snyder's craft book, *Save The Cat!*, or the *Save the Cat!* beat sheets online, to see what beats your ideal fan will want you to hit.

DONE LIST:

1. _____

2. _____

3. _____

CHECK-OUT:

Today's creative process flowed for me:

Not flowed **0 1 2 3 4 5 6 7 8 9 10** Totally flowed

Review your writing plans for tomorrow
and get psyched for **day five of writing!**

MY PLAN FOR NEXT WRITING BLOCK:

Date: _____

Time: _____

TO-DOS I WILL ACCOMPLISH:

1. _____ 3. _____

2. _____ 4. _____

TOOLS I PLAN TO USE IF I BECOME FRUSTRATED:

1. _____ 3. _____

2. _____ 4. _____

Knowing who you are writing for will help you make choices as you write and revise.

Pay attention to what emotions your fan will feel as they read through your project. The end goal is to make them feel what you want them to feel!

Author's Thank You Note: Thanks to **Sumi Gerry** for being a complete fan of my work and everything I do. I'm so lucky to have you in my life!

Fifth Day of Writing and Time is Currency

Day 11 Tasks: Day five of writing and build a time machine to find all the time in the world to write.

CHECK-IN:

I'm excited to create:

Not excited   **0 1 2 3 4 5 6 7 8 9 10**   Totally excited

I'm focused today:

Not focused   **0 1 2 3 4 5 6 7 8 9 10**   Totally focused

My Writing WHY: _____

Today, I'm grateful for: _____

Today, I forgive myself for: _____

Go ahead and write. When you've accomplished your goal, jot it down in your Done List, your plan for next block, reward yourself, and meet us back here!

★ **Great Job!** ★
You've WON your writing for today!

TODAY'S ACTIVITY TO WIN:
OPERATE WITH TIME AS CURRENCY AND TIME AUDIT

Everyone has the same amount of time in the day. When we examine what we do all day we're really looking at where we put our energy and focus.

It's important to put effort into things that you value. If you spend time doing things that you don't value as top priorities, there is a disconnect and negative feelings brew inside of you. Remember this as a tool to say yes to doing some things and no to others—without guilt.

We have to be protective of our time. This doesn't mean that we only work hard or value things that seem productive on the surface. There is a benefit to playing, for example, and if when we play, we feel less stressed, and can be more present in our lives, then there is value to that. Because the outcome of being more present is valuable, right?! Play is a coping mechanism. It may be a tool in your toolbox.

What happens when we let other people/things dictate how we spend our time? When we jump online to check email and then go down the rabbit hole of email or of Facebook or TED Talks or YouTube videos? We can spend hours on things we didn't plan on doing. We become reactive and passive instead of being in the driver's seat. At the end the day, we feel disconnected from our creativity and our goals.

We've already put this into practice a little—by listing our writing plans in our check-out section. If you develop a to-do list ahead of time based on your time priorities and goals then you have a solid direction for the day.

Another great way to deliberately pursue the things you value is to set time limits and use time cubes or timers on your phone to make sure that you're staying focused and not inadvertently internet surfing when you want to be writing.

Remember when we talked about how when you talk about writing, your brain thinks you have done the hard work of writing? Sometimes, we don't really know where we spend our time during the day.

Another great tool is a time audit.
For today, write down, on the following worksheet, what you work on for every fifteen minute time block. You may be surprised.

Author's Thank You Note: Thank you to **Kristine Asselin** for exemplifying professionalism as an author. Your ability to set goals and follow through and persevere through the hard writing times sets the highest bar to reach!

Worksheet 15: WIN AT TIME AUDITING

9:00	1:00	5:00
9:15	1:15	5:15
9:30	1:30	5:30
9:45	1:45	5:45
10:00	2:00	6:00
10:15	2:15	6:15
10:30	2:30	6:30
10:45	2:45	6:45
11:00	3:00	7:00
11:15	3:15	7:15
11:30	3:30	7:30
11:45	3:45	7:45
12:00	4:00	8:00
12:15	4:15	8:15
12:30	4:30	8:30
12:45	4:45	8:45

A word about things we can control and things we can't. There are times when unexpected things come up in our lives or our loved ones' lives and we must focus our time in a place we didn't plan. That's okay! Be kind to yourself and look forward to a time when you can jump back in to your creative project.

When you do work on what you planned to work on, and you spend your time currency on your creative project, you show yourself respect and prove you value your own worth. Pay yourself and your creativity first, and you will get creative dividends in no time!

Going forward, we will take a look at our values wheel, a tool to represent aspects of your life, which will allow us to put our energy into the things we value. We'll have a greater overall sense of peace in our lives and possibly find more time to write!

BONUS WIN: Search and watch Laura Vanderkam's TED Talk *How to Gain Control of Your Free Time*. She reminds us that time is a choice.

DONE LIST:

1. _____
2. _____
3. _____

CHECK-OUT:

Today's creative process flowed for me:

Not flowed **0 1 2 3 4 5 6 7 8 9 10** Totally flowed

**Review your writing plans for tomorrow
and get psyched for day six of writing!**

MY PLAN FOR NEXT WRITING BLOCK:

Date: _____

Time: _____

TO-DOS I WILL ACCOMPLISH:

1. _____   3. _____
2. _____   4. _____

TOOLS I PLAN TO USE IF I BECOME FRUSTRATED:

1. _____   3. _____
2. _____   4. _____

Sixth Day of Writing and Core Values Wheel

Day 12 Tasks: Your sixth day of writing and the day we talk about the values wheel.

CHECK-IN:

I'm excited to create:

Not excited **0 1 2 3 4 5 6 7 8 9 10** Totally excited

I'm focused today:

Not focused **0 1 2 3 4 5 6 7 8 9 10** Totally focused

My Writing WHY: _____

Today, I'm grateful for: _____

Today, I forgive myself for: _____

★ ★

★ **Have you Won the day? Jump down to the check-out and record** ★
that on your done list. And give yourself a reward!

★ ★

TODAY'S ACTIVITY TO WIN: ACKNOWLEDGE YOUR VALUES WHEEL

Hopefully, now you have gotten into the swing of things. You've enjoyed the serotonin boost of small successes each day and you're starting to ramp up to longer writing sessions. When you finish a session, you give yourself a small reward and then hang out with us so we can work more on nurturing our creativity.

I'm here to tell you something you already know.
You do not write in a vacuum. You create within a life that is
complicated and hopefully fulfilling.

There is this idea of creativity that you can fill the well with small random acts. Like, watch strangers going about their day and get inspired to write. Or watch a TED Talk, or listen to an inspiring podcast. Or go for a run. Or take a trip.

But I'm going to argue that these inspirations fit squarely into the values wheel, which we will take a look at now. It's very possible that your life is not all that balanced, and that's okay; we all start somewhere. But there is a real disconnect and negative feelings are produced when we spend time and energy on things that aren't valuable to us.

A piece of this idea is rooted in Maslow's Triangle or Hierarchy of Needs. The idea behind this psychological theory is that if you're focused on surviving you can't spend the time creating. So, if a part of your wheel of balance is starving, then it will be more difficult for you to create. Can you do it? Absolutely. Many people I know use writing as a creative lifeline to break out of life's hard moments. But if you aren't in crisis, you can nurture your creativity in long-term, sustaining ways.

So, today, let's take a look at the **Core Values Wheel of Balance:**

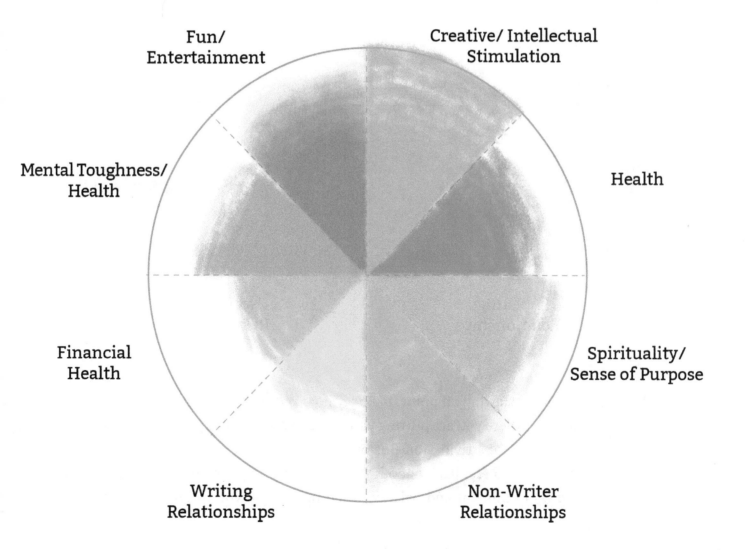

Let's take a look where we are starting. Shade in each pie section to the point that you feel like you are satisfied with how much energy you put into each value. If you shade a section in all the way, then you are confirming that section is just right, or ideal, for you. For example, if you have a ton of support from other writers and always have someone to turn to for answers about writerly questions, then you can fill in the Writing Relationships pie completely. If you only have one person who is in this writing journey with you, then just fill that pie in a little.

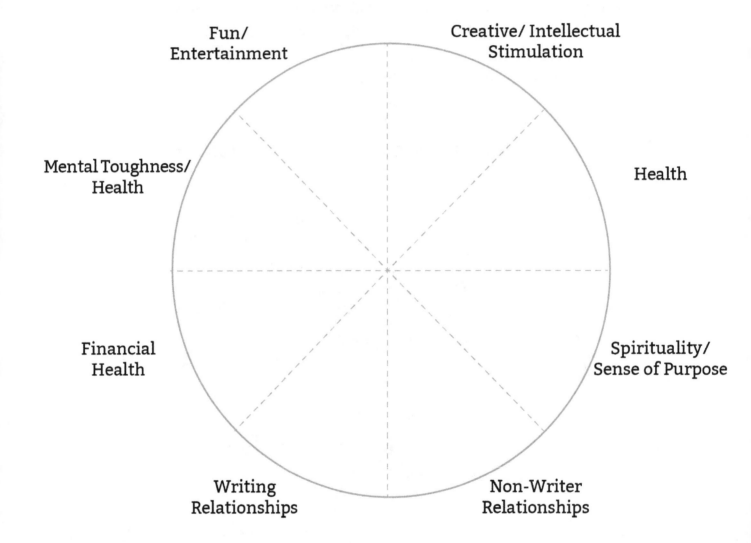

Remember, this is a starting off point. It's okay if you color in just a little of each pie. This is a way to look at where you are putting your time. Nobody has a perfectly balanced day; that is not what we are striving for. But over the course of a month or so, you can get to the point where you feel happy about where you spend your time and you can make choices based on fulfillment and balance when people ask you to give them your time and energy.

*It's a way to pay attention to what is important
and be deliberate about our time.*

BONUS WIN: Search for and watch Dan Thurmon's TED Talk *Off Balance on Purpose.*

DONE LIST:

1. _____
2. _____
3. _____

CHECK-OUT:

Today's creative process flowed for me:

Not flowed **0 1 2 3 4 5 6 7 8 9 10** Totally flowed

*Review your writing plans for tomorrow
and get psyched for **day seven of writing!***

MY PLAN FOR NEXT WRITING BLOCK:

Date: _____

Time: _____

TO-DOS I WILL ACCOMPLISH:

1. _____   3. _____
2. _____   4. _____

TOOLS I PLAN TO USE IF I BECOME FRUSTRATED:

1. _____   3. _____
2. _____   4. _____

Seventh Day of Writing and Core Values: Creative Stimulation

Day 13 Task: Your seventh day of writing and creative stimulation.

CHECK-IN:

I'm excited to create:

Not excited   **0 1 2 3 4 5 6 7 8 9 10**   Totally excited

I'm focused today:

Not focused   **0 1 2 3 4 5 6 7 8 9 10**   Totally focused

My Writing WHY: _____

Today, I'm grateful for: _____

Today, I forgive myself for: _____

Go write!

★   ★   **Yay!**   ★
★   **You've won another day!**   ★
★   ★

Fill in your check-out.

**Celebrate your success with a small reward!
Now we'll talk about filling our creative well.**

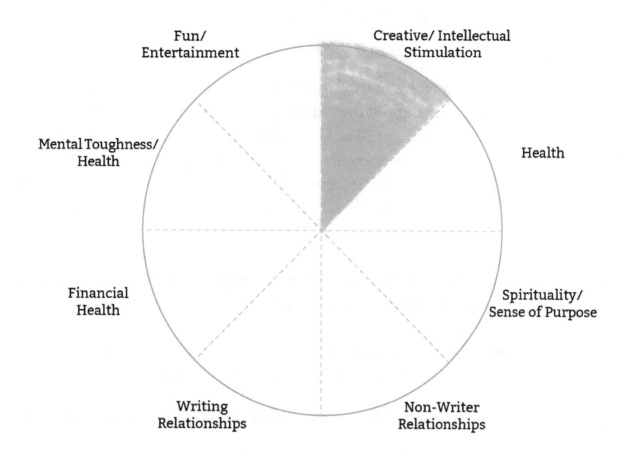

So, this is the easiest part of the pie right now, hopefully, since we're actively focusing on creating. You're spending a part of each day on creative stimulation with your writing.

Right now, let's prioritize what your most important aspect of creative stimulation is. If it is your writing, then we've already delved deeper into this and found your why. But maybe it's not. Maybe you are an author/illustrator and you want to prioritize practicing art as well.

My priority for creative stimulation in my life is: _____

_____

_____

_____

_____

_____

Day 13

Of course, some days will be easier than others.

If you feel as though the process of writing isn't filling your creative well, then turn to other creative acts to fill this up. Baking, knitting, and painting, etc. can fill the well. Dancing. Learning a new language. Watching movies and TV. Reading books. If done deliberately, these help you fill your creative well. Sometimes we need to do something new and different to spark creativity. Try a new creative venture. Play with paint or clay. Go to a museum. People-watch in a cafe. All this starts to move the part of our brain that says "what if."

You can also turn to others to connect with creative energy and intellectual stimulation. Watching TED Talks or YouTubers you love can make you think in new ways.

Talking with others about writing and creating can also fill this well if you feel depleted. Join a book club or talk to others about the creative aspects of your life.

List the ways that you love to fill your days or weeks with creative stimulation:

_____   _____

_____   _____

_____   _____

_____   _____

When we are feeling creatively depleted, we want to have a plan in place so we can act deliberately instead of react.

When I feel creatively low or burned out, my plan will be to take these steps:

_____   _____

_____   _____

_____   _____

_____   _____

BONUS WIN: Music is such a great muse! Search for music artist Lisa Hannigan on YouTube and watch how she mixes music with other creative practices—paper cutting, pop-up books, and other mixed media. **Get inspired!**

DONE LIST:

1. _____

2. _____

3. _____

CHECK-OUT:

Today's creative process flowed for me:

Not flowed   **0   1   2   3   4   5   6   7   8   9   10**   Totally flowed

Review your writing plans for tomorrow
and get psyched for **day eight of writing!**

MY PLAN FOR NEXT WRITING BLOCK:

Date: _____

Time: _____

TO-DOS I WILL ACCOMPLISH:

1. _____   3. _____

2. _____   4. _____

TOOLS I PLAN TO USE IF I BECOME FRUSTRATED:

1. _____   3. _____

2. _____   4. _____

Eighth Day of Writing and Core Values: Health

Day 14 Task: Eighth day of writing! And take stock of sleep, nutrition, and exercise habits.

CHECK-IN:

I'm excited to create:

Not excited   **0 1 2 3 4 5 6 7 8 9 10**   Totally excited

I'm focused today:

Not focused   **0 1 2 3 4 5 6 7 8 9 10**   Totally focused

My Writing WHY: _____

Today, I'm grateful for: _____

Today, I forgive myself for: _____

Now go write!

You nailed it, right?!
Won the day! Take a moment to give yourself a small reward so your brain recognizes how awesome it is to write!

Fill in your check-out. Now we'll talk about our overall health.

TODAY'S ACTIVITY TO WIN: FOCUS ON YOUR HEALTH

Health is something that feeds the creative well. If our bodies don't feel great, we won't feel like creating.

But we also know that we can't change EVERYTHING all at once. While working through this manual, we're putting our writing habit on project status. We don't want to derail that by focusing too much on our healthy habits, but let's just take a moment to think about how we value our health and how our choices reflect the respect we feel for our bodies.

When I'm tired or on a sugar high, it is so hard for me to get my brain working properly. I get some of my best ideas for writing while I'm walking. Something about movement helps my ideas and words move forward too.

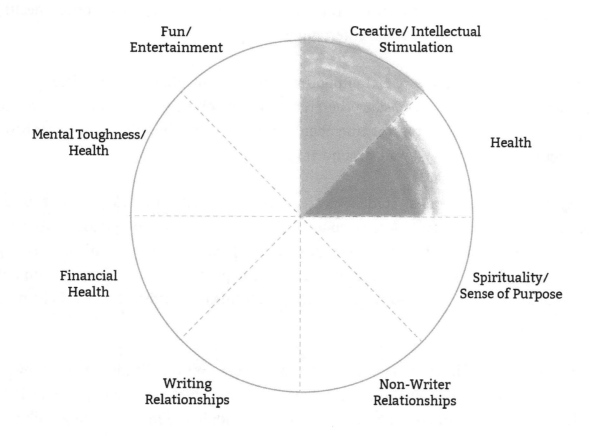

What do you value most about being healthy? Is it a good night's sleep? Is it moving your body? Is it eating nutritious foods? _____

_____

_____

_____

_____

_____

_____

_____

When we act in accordance with our values, we experience less emotional and intellectual discord. When you have a choice of where to put your time, remember what is on the top of your list for healthy living. It's even more powerful to combine your top values around the wheel. For instance, my priorities include spending time with my family and having fun. So playing a game outside with my kids fills in all those pie spaces at once—health, non-writer relationships, and fun/entertainment.

For writers, healthy habits are extra important because hunching over your desk writing isn't good for your body. Consider the ergonomics involved with writing and how to improve them. One easy thing to remember to do while you're building your writer habit is to get up and stretch and walk around at intervals.

Sleeping Tips and Tricks: Studies have shown that playing a quick puzzle game on your phone thirty minutes before sleep untangles and stops the thought loops from the day. Those thoughts that tend to keep you up and become worries at night. Wearing glasses that block the blue light (since blue light suppresses your natural melatonin) before bed is helpful. Going to bed and getting up at the same time every day is helpful.

Exercise Tips: Work while standing if you can, or get up from sitting often and move around. When you are going after your BONUS WIN, which is normally a TED Talk, podcast, or another form of multimedia, plug your headphones in and go for a walk or a run while listening. If you get book ideas, text yourself, or write in a digital note on your phone!

Nutrition Tips: Make nutrition easy on yourself. If you aren't a cook, get frozen dinners of healthful food that you can whip up quickly for yourself or your family. Make your food choices just a slightly healthier version of what you are used to eating and it will go far to help you feel better. And just like how we plan ahead what we are writing in the next writing block, plan what your next snack or meal will be. Having a plan keeps you on track!

This is an opportunity to think about what you value most regarding your health. Thinking about what you value and making your choices and values line up makes your life is less discordant

BONUS WIN: If you want to go deeper into this thought of the healthy writer, check out Joanna Penn's book The Healthy Writer: Reduce Your Pain, Improve Your Health, and Build a Writing Career For The Long Term. (It's available as an audiobook in case you want to listen to it on a walk!)

DONE LIST:

1. _____

2. _____

3. _____

CHECK-OUT:

Today's creative process flowed for me:

Not flowed **0 1 2 3 4 5 6 7 8 9 10** Totally flowed

Review your writing plans for tomorrow
and get psyched for **day nine of writing!**

MY PLAN FOR NEXT WRITING BLOCK:

Date: _____

Time: _____

TO-DOS I WILL ACCOMPLISH:

1. _____   3. _____

2. _____   4. _____

TOOLS I PLAN TO USE IF I BECOME FRUSTRATED:

1. _____   3. _____

2. _____   4. _____

Ninth Day of Writing and Core Values: Spirituality/Sense of Purpose

Day 16 Tasks: Ninth day of writing! And discover your purpose in the universe!

CHECK-IN:

I'm excited to create:

Not excited **0 1 2 3 4 5 6 7 8 9 10** Totally excited

I'm focused today:

Not focused **0 1 2 3 4 5 6 7 8 9 10** Totally focused

My Writing WHY: _____

Today, I'm grateful for: _____

Today, I forgive myself for: _____

★   ★

Go ahead and get that writing done!
You WIN! Then give yourself a reward
and come on back here!

TODAY'S ACTIVITY TO WIN: SENSE OF PURPOSE

One reason why we look at the values wheel while we're building our creative habits, is to have it in the back of our head as we say "yes" and "no" to things in our life. When we put our time and effort into things that don't fit into our values wheel, we experience disconnect and negative feelings.

When we talk about spirituality and sense of purpose, we're talking about what values we hold in high esteem. We're talking about what is most important to us, morally, and how we feel interconnected to the people in our community and world.

It's hard to say "no" to someone or something. But if we are already saying "yes" to tasks that align with our personality and sense of purpose, then we can say "no" to those non-valued tasks without feeling guilty.

Volunteering and lending our time in a way that feeds our spirituality strengthens our sense of purpose and connectedness. And it gives us permission to not do things that we don't feel correlate to our values.

It lets us set our priorities, and put our time into those things that are most important to us. When we feel at peace with where we are spending our time, we nurture our souls, and are more inspired to create.

Think about how you want to move around in the world and try to cast off thinking about how others live around you. Think about doing things that are important to you and not getting tied up in things that you don't value or have time for. This connects you more meaningfully to your family, your friends, your school/religious center/town community, your surroundings, and to the world.

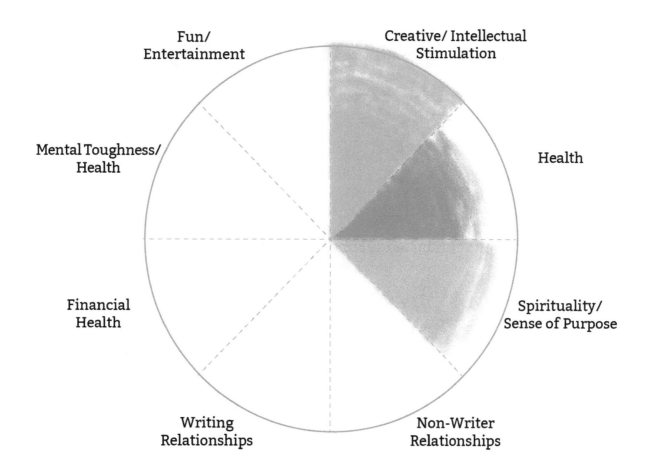

Worksheet 16: WIN at Aligning My Values

My priorities:

1. _____
2. _____
3. _____
4. _____
5. _____

Things I want to say yes to, that align with my values:

1. _____
2. _____
3. _____
4. _____
5. _____

Things I want to set boundaries around/say no to:

1. _____
2. _____
3. _____
4. _____
5. _____

BONUS WIN: When we are most connected with ourselves, we are most connected to what we value. Try Julia Cameron's Morning Pages, by writing three pages of stream of consciousness, without censoring. Just write whatever comes to mind! For a deeper dive, check out her book, The Artist's Way.

DONE LIST:

1. _____

2. _____

3. _____

CHECK-OUT:

Today's creative process flowed for me:

Not flowed   **0   1   2   3   4   5   6   7   8   9   10**   Totally flowed

**Review your writing plans for tomorrow
and get psyched for day ten of writing!**

MY PLAN FOR NEXT WRITING BLOCK:

Date: _____

Time: _____

TO-DOS I WILL ACCOMPLISH:

1. _____   3. _____

2. _____   4. _____

TOOLS I PLAN TO USE IF I BECOME FRUSTRATED:

1. _____   3. _____

2. _____   4. _____

Tenth Day of Writing and Core Values: Non-Writing Relationships

Day 16 Task: Think about how to be supported in creative ventures by your non-writing support system. And your tenth writing day!

CHECK-IN:

I'm excited to create:

       Not excited   **0 1 2 3 4 5 6 7 8 9 10** Totally excited

I'm focused today:

       Not focused   **0 1 2 3 4 5 6 7 8 9 10** Totally focusedd

My Writing WHY: _____

Today, I'm grateful for: _____

Today, I forgive myself for: _____

You've been writing for ten days! GO you. Go write.

⭐ **Now that You've Won the day, give yourself a reward.** ⭐

TODAY'S ACTIVITY TO WIN: NON-WRITING RELATIONSHIPS

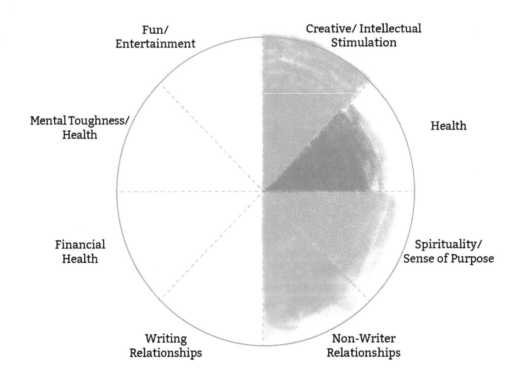

Fun/ Entertainment

Creative/ Intellectual Stimulation

Mental Toughness/ Health

Health

Financial Health

Spirituality/ Sense of Purpose

Writing Relationships

Non-Writer Relationships

We don't live in a world surrounded only by writers or people who know what writing is like. The people closest to us might not really understand.

One of the most important parts of writing is to convey to the friends and family who love us that this journey, as painful as it can be, feeds us.

As we dedicate time to a pursuit that may not have immediate results, it's important for us to help the people around us know that the journey is worthwhile, and we must create boundaries around our writing time.

It's also important for us to be able to talk coherently about our work.

You'll need a pitch, for anyone who asks what you are working on. It should be a few sentences. You've worked on this back on **Worksheet 6**. It's time to solidify your pitch so you can use it to answer the question, "What are you writing?"

If you need help in sharpening your pitch, check out the blurbs of books similar to yours and write in that vein. You can also check out resources about building pitches from experts like The Book Doctors, Arielle Eckstut and David Henry Sterry, and their book, The Essential Guide to Getting Your Book Published.

Take your pitch from **Worksheet 6** and rework it until you feel comfortable with it.

Revamped Pitch: _____

_____

_____

_____

_____

_____

_____

It's also important that people around you have a realistic expectation for how long you will be working on this project. Writing can take a long time. And if you're pursuing traditional publishing, it's important to convey the amount of time it might take before you see your project published.

If you have a significant other or children, you may want to share your goals with them. Where you want to be at the end of the year. Where you see your career going in five years. People who love you want to support you and want to know how.

You are the one to give them that understanding.

For family and friends who don't see you work every day on your writing, it's good to develop another type of answer to the question, "How's your writing coming along?"

When asked this question, I am vague but upbeat, because people will follow my tone.

SETTING BOUNDARIES

Be prepared. When people know that you are a writer, they will start to ask you for free writing help. I've really enjoyed helping teens write essays for private schools and colleges. I've helped write content for friends' and relatives' websites. But I choose, very carefully, who I say "yes" to about helping. Sometimes I ask for a trade: "I'll help you if you help me with something in your skillset." And sometimes I point someone in the direction of other help because I can't spare the time.

It's up to you to set boundaries!

Author's Thank You Note: Thank you to **Michaela McDonald** for supporting me and my work even when I wasn't supporting my work. For always giving me perspective and cheering me on!

Author's Thank You Note: Thank you to **Arielle Eckstut** and **David Henry Sterry** for all the support they've given me through the years and the support they continue to give writers wading through the weeds of pitching and getting published.

BONUS WIN: Scott Dinsmore, in his TED Talk, *How to Find Work You Love*, says that eighty percent of people hate their jobs. Watch his talk and let it give you the ammunition to talk meaningfully about writing with the people who may not understand it fully!

DONE LIST:

1. _____

2. _____

3. _____

CHECK-OUT:

Today's creative process flowed for me:

   Not flowed   **0 1 2 3 4 5 6 7 8 9 10**   Totally flowed

**Review your writing plans for tomorrow
and get psyched for day eleven of writing!**

MY PLAN FOR NEXT WRITING BLOCK:

Date: _____

Time: _____

TO-DOS I WILL ACCOMPLISH:

1. _____   3. _____

2. _____   4. _____

TOOLS I PLAN TO USE IF I BECOME FRUSTRATED:

1. _____   3. _____

2. _____   4. _____

Eleventh Day of Writing and Core Values: Writing Relationships

Day 17 Task: Writing day eleven and focus on your writing support system.

CHECK-IN:

I'm excited to create:

       Not excited   **0 1 2 3 4 5 6 7 8 9 10**   Totally excited

I'm focused today:

       Not focused   **0 1 2 3 4 5 6 7 8 9 10**   Totally focused

My Writing WHY: _____

Today, I'm grateful for: _____

Today, I forgive myself for: _____

★ ★
Write first, reward yourself for **WINNING THE DAY!**
and then come back for today's next win!

We're keeping the activities short and sweet so that you can spend most of your time on your creative venture.

TODAY'S ACTIVITY TO WIN: FIND YOUR PEOPLE

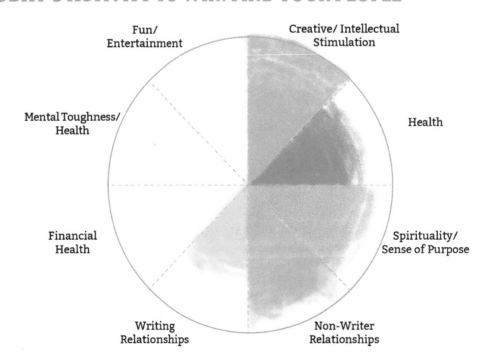

Fun/
Entertainment

Creative/ Intellectual
Stimulation

Mental Toughness/
Health

Health

Financial
Health

Spirituality/
Sense of Purpose

Writing
Relationships

Non-Writer
Relationships

Creative careers are tough.
It's important to surround yourself with people who
WILL NOT LET YOU FAIL.

Throughout your writing career, you will probably have many connections in the writing community like:

Mentors and people further along on the path you want to walk

Critique partners who help you brainstorm and solve creative problems

Teachers of online or in-person courses, and authors of writing craft books you utilize

Friends who emotionally support you and bring fun and happiness into your writing life

With social media, it is easier than ever, but just as important, to find people who have common interests and goals. Join a group that is working on projects similar to those that you are. Be supportive of others and ask what you can do for them. Those same people will likely be supportive of you when you have a need.

Below, list five ways you could find writers who are on a journey like yours. It could be going to a conference or taking a class at a local college. You could join a social media group and join in the conversation. It could be listening to a new podcast. Even though that seems passive, you'll feel like you're a part of that podcaster's community. Leave the podcaster a comment telling them what their words, inspiration, and information mean to you.

Five ways I can build my writing community:

1. _____

2. _____

3. _____

4. _____

5. _____

BONUS WIN: Dive into the world of the podcasting community! Check out Write Now with Sarah Rhea Werner, The Creative Writer's Toolbelt with Andrew J Chamberlain, or Magic Lessons with Elizabeth Gilbert.

DONE LIST:

1. _____

2. _____

3. _____

CHECK-OUT:

Today's creative process flowed for me:

Not flowed **0 1 2 3 4 5 6 7 8 9 10** Totally flowed

Review your writing plans for tomorrow
and get psyched for day **twelve of writing!**

MY PLAN FOR NEXT WRITING BLOCK:

Date: _____

Time: _____

TO-DOS I WILL ACCOMPLISH:

1. _____   3. _____

2. _____   4. _____

TOOLS I PLAN TO USE IF I BECOME FRUSTRATED:

1. _____   3. _____

2. _____   4. _____

Author's Thank You Note: Thank you to **Warren Ross** for always lifting me up and inspiring me to be my most creative self. Thanks for walking the walk, Warren, and showing me how it's done!

We'll talk more about community and collaboration in later sections, so continue to think about finding your people and building your writing support.

Author's Thank You Note: Thank you to the amazing NE-SCBWI leaders who taught me how to build community through running conferences: **Margo Lemieux**, **Sally Riley**, and **Marilyn Salerno**. It takes a village and it takes excellent leadership to keep that village strong! I don't know where I'd be without you three!

Twelfth Day of Writing and Core Values: Financial Wins

Day 18 Task: Writing day twelve and focus on finances.

CHECK-IN:

I'm excited to create:

Not excited **0 1 2 3 4 5 6 7 8 9 10** Totally excited

I'm focused today:

Not focused **0 1 2 3 4 5 6 7 8 9 10** Totally focused

My Writing WHY: _____

Today, I'm grateful for: _____

Today, I forgive myself for: _____

★ **WIN at writing** and then come back and do your check-out! ★
Make sure to reward yourself!

TODAY'S ACTIVITY TO WIN: SET YOURSELF UP FOR FINANCIAL WIN

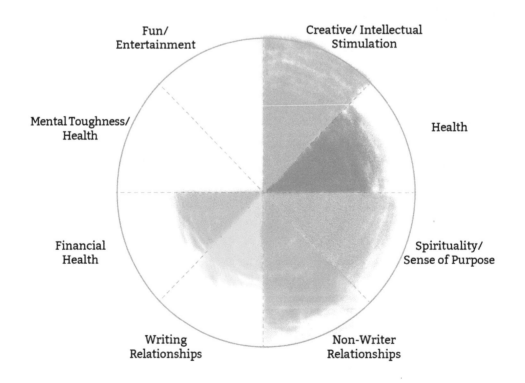

Sometimes putting on the business hat as an author can be daunting. It's tempting to be a writing recluse and ignore the business side of things. It can be exciting, though. You are creating works of intellectual property that will go out into the world and make money for you.

I assume you have some source of income to sustain you—likely have a day job that brings money into the household. You might love that job and plan on keeping it while you write on the side.

But for some, you might want writing to be your primary source of income. Most writers who do this have multiple creative streams of revenue. They lead workshops at conferences and online, they do author visits, they counsel other writers, they have multiple books in multiple forms for purchase (e-book, paperback, audio), or they have podcasts. And they market themselves.

Right now, you may be considering some of these avenues. Or you might be trying to get through writing your first project.

The important thing is to focus on financial independence or FI—a movement with three simple pillars:

1. Spend less.

2. Make more.

3. Invest.

Just because you are a writer doesn't mean you can't be great at finances and the business end of your life. Although, I often hear, "I'm a writer; my brain doesn't work that way."

You can learn it all from people in the financial field, or hire someone whose brain does work that way to give you advice or help you manage investments and taxes.

Just like with our time audit, I recommend looking at where you spend your money and whether those areas reflect your values.

Fill out **Worksheet 17** so you have a clear picture of where you spend your money.

Worksheet 17: WIN the Financial Audit   Page 1

Itemize and total your last month's expenses. Group things together, so if you visit Starbucks fifteen times, enter that total on a line in Food and Drink Expenses as one total. Then total up each block.

Month:

Food and Drink Expenses

			Total:

Clothing Expenses

			Total:

Utility Expenses (rent/mortgate/utilites)

			Total:

Technology Expenses (cable, phones)

			Total:

Health Expenses

			Total:

Entertainment and Fun Expenses

			Total:

Travel

			Total:

Business Expenses

			Total:

Other

			Total:

BONUS WIN: Check out Joanna Penn's The Creative Penn podcast interview with Brad Barrett of ChooseFI. If you're an indie publisher, check out the Facebook group 20 Books to 50K.

BONUS BONUS WIN:

Check out the podcast *WELCOME TO THE FI COMMUNITY* with Brad Barrett and Jonathan Mendonsa. Choose episode 100.

DONE LIST:

1. _____

2. _____

3. _____

CHECK-OUT:

Today's creative process flowed for me:

Not flowed **0 1 2 3 4 5 6 7 8 9 10** Totally flowed

Review your writing plans for tomorrow
and get psyched for **day thirteen of writing!**

MY PLAN FOR NEXT WRITING BLOCK:

Date: _____

Time: _____

TO-DOS I WILL ACCOMPLISH:

1. _____   3. _____

2. _____   4. _____

TOOLS I PLAN TO USE IF I BECOME FRUSTRATED:

1. _____   3. _____

2. _____   4. _____

"Risk is essential. It's scary. Every time I sit down and start the first page of a novel I am risking failure. We are encouraged in this world not to fail...I think that is a bad thing that the world has done to us...We are encouraged only to do that which we can be successful in. But things are accomplished only by our risk of failure. Writers will never do anything beyond the first thing unless they risk growing."

–Madeleine L'Engle (Herself 2001)

Thirteenth Day of Writing and Core Values: Mental Toughness/Health

Day 19 Task: You've been writing for nearly two weeks! Today you'll write and protect mental toughness.

CHECK-IN:

I'm excited to create:

Not excited **0 1 2 3 4 5 6 7 8 9 10** Totally excited

I'm focused today:

Not focused **0 1 2 3 4 5 6 7 8 9 10** Totally focused

My Writing WHY: _____

Today, I'm grateful for: _____

Today, I forgive myself for: _____

Go get your writing done.

★ ★
Bask in the glow of your success!
★ **Give yourself a treat and then come back here to work through another** ★
★ **aspect of being a healthy creative.** ★

TODAY'S ACTIVITY TO WIN: BUILD UP MENTAL TOUGHNESS

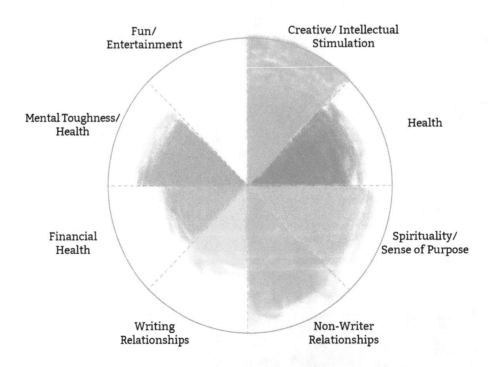

Fun/Entertainment · Creative/Intellectual Stimulation · Mental Toughness/Health · Health · Financial Health · Spirituality/Sense of Purpose · Writing Relationships · Non-Writer Relationships

Most often we only focus on our mental health or mental toughness when we are already feeling low or anxious. Being proactive and doing something every day to help us cope with stress is important. Developing great coping skills and using them even when times aren't tough helps us stay resilient.

Being creative can make us even more vulnerable. We take the innermost part of our selves, express it in a way we hope others can connect to, and put it out on display. We open ourselves up for criticism. We invite others into our most personal thoughts and worlds.

Depression and anxiety are not uncommon for creative types. We live inside our heads and scrutinize what's in there. If you are having trouble living your life because of anxiety or depression, make sure to find someone professional to support you.

For passing thoughts, there are secrets to allowing them to pass by—for us to not get tripped up by them.

Remember that toolbox that we stocked on day seven? Let's revisit that and make sure that we're using tools to combat negative thoughts and emotions. Remember, an emotion only physiologically lives for ninety seconds. If your emotions are lasting longer, then you are sustaining them.

So, list the top five tools you are using to combat negative emotions. List only those that you have used that have worked for you.

1. _____

2. _____

3. _____

4. _____

5. _____

Were they the same tools you thought you would use?

If your tools aren't working as well as you'd hoped, here's a chance to pick new tools and try them out. Revisit the list of tools in **Day 7** for ideas.

Tip: Puzzles can be a quick way to unravel negative loops of thinking. Spending a few moments stacking candies or threading flowers together or Sudoku-ing can break a worry loop.

Tip: Fresh air and sun can work wonders. For people who live in cold climates, blue light can ward off the effects of seasonal affective disorder.

Tip: Take your gratitude one step further. Tell someone (in an email, on the phone, or in a note—it doesn't matter the method) that you are grateful for them. It'll boost your positive emotions.

Anxious and depressive thoughts are a product of stress. And believe it or not, stress doesn't have to be a bad thing.

Check out the bonus wins to find out how to have
a healthier relationship with stress and anxiety!

BONUS WIN: Watch the TED Talk *How to Make Stress Your Friend*, with Kelly McGonigal. (If she seems familiar, she's the twin sister of TED Talker Jane McGonigal!)

BONUS BONUS WIN: It's been shown that the elite athletes like Olympians experience anxiety before a big event as excitement. You can train yourself to do so as well! Read the article, How To Channel Your Nerves For Success Like An Olympic Athlete on elitedaily. com and check out the article's reference links!

Author's Thank You Note: A big thanks to **Sandy Budiansky** for showing me what true mental toughness looks like. I'm in awe of your ability to positively march through any barriers in your way!

DONE LIST:

1. _____

2. _____

3. _____

CHECK-OUT:

Today's creative process flowed for me:

Not flowed **0 1 2 3 4 5 6 7 8 9 10** Totally flowed

Review your writing plans for tomorrow
and get psyched for **day fourteen of writing!**

MY PLAN FOR NEXT WRITING BLOCK:

Date: _____

Time: _____

TO-DOS I WILL ACCOMPLISH:

1. _____ 3. _____

2. _____ 4. _____

TOOLS I PLAN TO USE IF I BECOME FRUSTRATED:

1. _____ 3. _____

2. _____ 4. _____

Fourteenth Day of Writing and Core Values: Fun

Day 20 Tasks: Write and have some fun!

CHECK-IN:

I'm excited to create:

Not excited   **0 1 2 3 4 5 6 7 8 9 10**   Totally excited

I'm focused today:

Not focused   **0 1 2 3 4 5 6 7 8 9 10**   Totally focused

My Writing WHY: _____

Today, I'm grateful for: _____

Today, I forgive myself for: _____

After today, you've hit the two-weeks-mark of solid writing! Just one more week to go before you've made it a habit!

★   ★   ★

★ **Get that writing done so you WIN the day!** ★

★   ★

TODAY'S ACTIVITY TO WIN: HAVE FUN!

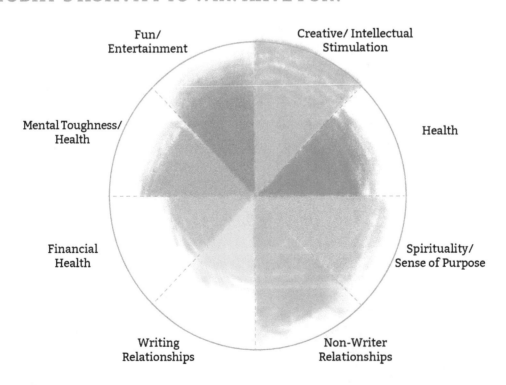

Fun/Entertainment

Creative/Intellectual Stimulation

Mental Toughness/Health

Health

Financial Health

Spirituality/Sense of Purpose

Writing Relationships

Non-Writer Relationships

We've talked about forgiveness and being grateful. We've talked about finding happiness along the journey, rather than succumbing to the if-then predicament where we never get to actually experience being happy.

There is joy in the journey. There is joy in the learning of new ways to spin a story and new ways to reach fans. There is joy in making mistakes and then learning to make new ones. There is joy in sharing a story for the first time with critique partners or editors and there is a lot of joy in typing "The End."

Fun and adventures feed the writing. Those experiences can give perspective and new magic to bring into your writing.

But when the process doesn't feel like fun, when we think that what we are doing is not worthy of joy, we can look for fun outside of the creative process as well.

Think about going out and finding something fun to do. Too often, as adults, we skip this part of the values wheel. We know we have to do the hard work. But just as important is doing the fun stuff. It shifts our perspective and recharges our creative batteries.

Laughing is an excellent way to change perspective.

Make time for play. Make time for fun. Just as you would make time for doing the hard work.

Author's Thank You Note: Thank you to **Bob Thibeault** for bringing fun into the work. I love leaning on your amazing ideas and brilliance—the possibilities of collaboration with you keeps me creating!

This week go find some fun.
Field trip time!

Here's my fun list:

1. _____

2. _____

3. _____

4. _____

5. _____

6. _____

7. _____

8. _____

9. _____

10. _____

BONUS WIN: Learn how to find the fun in whatever mundane tasks you're doing! Check out the TED Talk *The Agony of Trying to Unsubscribe* with James Veitch. Super funny.

DONE LIST:

1. _____

2. _____

3. _____

CHECK-OUT:

Today's creative process flowed for me:

Not flowed **0 1 2 3 4 5 6 7 8 9 10** Totally flowed

**Review your writing plans for tomorrow
and get psyched for day fifteen of writing!**

MY PLAN FOR NEXT WRITING BLOCK:

Date: _____

Time: _____

TO-DOS I WILL ACCOMPLISH:

1. _____ 3. _____

2. _____ 4. _____

TOOLS I PLAN TO USE IF I BECOME FRUSTRATED:

1. _____ 3. _____

2. _____ 4. _____

Fifteenth Day of Writing and Building Community

Day 21 Tasks: Write and think about building support into your community

CHECK-IN:

I'm excited to create:

Not excited   **0 1 2 3 4 5 6 7 8 9 10**   Totally excited

I'm focused today:

Not focused   **0 1 2 3 4 5 6 7 8 9 10**   Totally focused

My Writing WHY: _____

Today, I'm grateful for: _____

Today, I forgive myself for: _____

Have you WON the day with your writing? Reward yourself, and ride high on the feeling of success!

TODAY'S ACTIVITY TO WIN: BUILD YOUR COMMUNITY

We've touched on this point a little bit when we were talking about nurturing relationships with other writers in the values wheel.

Bottom line: Your writing product will be better if you have a strong writing community to support you. Why? Because it's hard to know what you'll need next (we'll talk more about this later!).

So, let's talk about the type of writing support you need, and how to get it.

1. Knowledge. There's always room to learn and grow. We can find this type of support through reading craft books and taking classes or workshops, online, or at conferences.

2. Emotional Support. We need cheerleaders. People to say, "Hey, creating is tough, but you can do it." Non-writers can give this to you as well, of course, but the people who know what you are going through the best are the people in the creative trenches with you.

3. Feedback. Whether it's an editor we've hired, if we are indie-publishing, or a critique partner, we need to find feedback to give us perspective. You can find critique groups locally by joining writer groups or online.

4. Shared Resources. This is where writers share their knowledge on the business side of things. Good agents and editors, good for-hire editors and cover artists. We can find these groups online and locally. Shared resources can also be shared email lists and access to fans.

5. Accountability. We tend to be more efficient when we have deadlines and people keeping us to our deadlines. When we have to answer to someone about whether we are getting our own goals accomplished. We get more words written when we do writing sprints alongside other writers (virtually or in-person) and get more accomplished when we know that someone is keeping tabs on our progress.

Author's Thank You Note: Thank you to author **Erin Dionne** for knitting community together at the Writers' Loft through her workshops, classes, and insight on the Board. She is a master community builder and I always seek out her measured and gracious guidance!

Worksheet 18: WIN at Building My Community   Page 1

Brainstorm who can help you in each area of community. If you need to find someone to fit a category, brainstorm where you might connect with them.

1. Knowledge

2. Emotional Support

3. Feedback

4. Shared Resources

5. Accountability

Day 21

When you are seeking community, the best thing to do is to ask "What can I do for you?" instead of looking immediately for what you can get from others. You want to develop a relationship rather than just have a one-time demand.

You may wonder how to find people to build your community. This manual has already been adding people to your community. Through podcasts, TED Talks, and other resources, you have been introduced to people in the business. You can dig a little deeper and go to Joanna Penn's website, for example, and then seek out her Facebook group or blog, or wherever people are gathering with her to talk about writing.

You can find community locally, too. Most likely there is a writing conference or retreat, relating to your genre, happening somewhere near you. Your local indie bookseller might know of some writing groups in your area. Or you can take a writing class locally or online. In that class, you will definitely find other writers.

BONUS WIN: Check out the online database my friend Dominic Perri started to help writers to find community wherever they are. It's at www.hollihock.com. The tag line is "Find your place." Use it to find your place in the local writing community!

Author's Thank You Note: Thanks to **Dom Perri** and **Kelsey Knoedler** for building amazing communities and opportunities for authors. I love all your big ideas and will always champion you two!

DONE LIST:

1. _____

2. _____

3. _____

CHECK-OUT:

Today's creative process flowed for me:

Not flowed   **0 1 2 3 4 5 6 7 8 9 10**   Totally flowed

Review your writing plans for tomorrow
and get psyched for **day sixteen of writing!**

MY PLAN FOR NEXT WRITING BLOCK:

Date: _____

Time: _____

TO-DOS I WILL ACCOMPLISH:

1. _____   3. _____

2. _____   4. _____

TOOLS I PLAN TO USE IF I BECOME FRUSTRATED:

1. _____   3. _____

2. _____   4. _____

Sixteenth Day of Writing and Writing When You're Stuck

Day 22 Task: Write and write, no matter how you're feeling about it.

CHECK-IN:

I'm excited to create:

       Not excited **0 1 2 3 4 5 6 7 8 9 10** Totally excited

I'm focused today:

       Not focused **0 1 2 3 4 5 6 7 8 9 10** Totally focused

My Writing WHY: _____

Today, I'm grateful for: _____

Today, I forgive myself for: _____

★ Have you WON the day with your writing? Go do that, reward yourself, and ride high on the feeling of success!

TODAY'S ACTIVITY TO WIN: WRITING WHEN STUCK

Sometimes when we get stuck it's not about creativity or barriers to sitting down to do the writing--sometimes we don't know what to do next in our project.

You've tried to use your toolboxes and realize that you are in the right frame of mind and emotion to write. You've carved out time to write. You just don't know how to work forward in your project.

While this is a larger subject that is covered in other Creatively WIN workbooks, you might need to tackle it a bit during this workbook.

What happens when you don't know how to work forward on your project?

You've got your to-do list and plan. You know that you need to write 1000 words or revise for an hour, but you don't know how to write or revise the content.

Or you believe you don't know.

If you are writing because you love storytelling then you need to trust yourself to trust your instinct.

And you need to trust that if you don't have the tools to keep working forward, then you can find where to get them.

It may be finding a mentor text (something that is similar to your project in genre and already published) or going back to think about your character's arc if you are writing fiction. If you are revising, you may need to get feedback from someone who has perspective on your writing to find out what works and what doesn't.

The main thing is to figure out how to get back into production mode as quickly as possible.

Some possible techniques:

1. Reread the work you did on your last writing or revising day and see if that gives you enough of a blueprint to move forward.

2. Outline your story and see if that helps you discover a what to do next.

3. Hold a brainstorming session with yourself—this could focus on characters, plot, or worldbuilding.

4. Watch a show or movie in a similar genre to your book. It may unlock things and can be easier to synthesize story in a visual medium.

5. Find a mentor text (a published work similar in genre to your product) and read it.

6. Soundboard off another writer. Describe where you are in your story and many times you will talk through the solution yourself.

7. Allow yourself to lower your standards so you can get this version of the story out.

Day 22

BONUS WIN: Check out Elizabeth Gilbert's TED Talk *Your Elusive Creative Genius*.

BONUS BONUS WIN: Check out Sean Platt, Johnny B. Truant, and David Wright in their StoryShop podcast. They'll show you how they first figure out the broad strokes of putting the story into an outline and then go through and write each scene.

DONE LIST:

1. _____
2. _____
3. _____

CHECK-OUT:

Today's creative process flowed for me:

Not flowed **0 1 2 3 4 5 6 7 8 9 10** Totally flowed

**Review your writing plans for tomorrow
and get psyched for day seventeen of writing!**

MY PLAN FOR NEXT WRITING BLOCK:

Date: _____

Time: _____

TO-DOS I WILL ACCOMPLISH:

1. _____ 3. _____
2. _____ 4. _____

TOOLS I PLAN TO USE IF I BECOME FRUSTRATED:

1. _____ 3. _____
2. _____ 4. _____

"Writing and reading decrease our sense of isolation. They deepen and widen and expand our sense of life: they feed the soul.
When writers make us shake our heads with the exactness of their prose and their truths, and even make us laugh about ourselves or life, our buoyancy is restored."

–Anne Lamott, Bird by Bird

Seventeenth Day of Writing and Writing Core

Day 23 Task: Write and use a core to hang your writing on. For most writers, this is reflected in themes.

CHECK-IN:

I'm excited to create:

        Not excited   **0 1 2 3 4 5 6 7 8 9 10**   Totally excited

I'm focused today:

        Not focused   **0 1 2 3 4 5 6 7 8 9 10**   Totally focused

My Writing WHY: _____

Today, I'm grateful for: _____

Today, I forgive myself for: _____

Have you WON the day with your writing? Go do that, reward yourself, and ride high on the feeling of success!

TODAY'S ACTIVITY TO WIN: IDENTIFY YOUR WRITING CORE

Now, take a look at all your manuscripts, books, or ideas.
What are the common threads across them?

Every writer works within some signature themes, that you can spot across their books. They might be themes like family ties, protecting those you love, finding one's truth, etc. When you spot what your general themes are as an author, it helps you know what the important facets are of the projects you are working on. You may have different overarching themes if you work in different genres.

Now, if you consider the project you're working on now, you can get a little more specific. There is a core to your story—something that relates to your theme—and if it wasn't there, your story would fall apart. You may not know what this is until after your first draft, but knowing the core of your story is essential for revisions.

Take a moment and think about what the core of your current project may be. Even just thinking about what is at the heart of your story will help as you work forward.

The core of my story is: _____
_____
_____
_____
_____
_____
_____

Knowing your overarching themes that you like to explore through your writing is essential to understanding your brand and how to market yourself as an author, which we will talk about in the next section.

BONUS WIN: Check out John Truby's book *The Anatomy of Story: 22 Steps to Becoming a Master Storyteller* and delve deeper into your signature creative style.

CHECK-OUT:

Today's creative process flowed for me:

Not flowed **0 1 2 3 4 5 6 7 8 9 10** Totally flowed

Review your writing plans for tomorrow
and get psyched for **day eighteen of writing!**

MY PLAN FOR NEXT WRITING BLOCK:

Date: _____

Time: _____

TO-DOS I WILL ACCOMPLISH:

1. _____   3. _____

2. _____   4. _____

TOOLS I PLAN TO USE IF I BECOME FRUSTRATED:

1. _____   3. _____

2. _____   4. _____

Eighteenth Day of Writing and My Career Brand

Day 24 Tasks: Write and think of how to present your professional self to the world!

CHECK-IN:

I'm excited to create:

Not excited **0 1 2 3 4 5 6 7 8 9 10** Totally excited

I'm focused today:

Not focused **0 1 2 3 4 5 6 7 8 9 10** Totally focused

My Writing WHY: _____

Today, I'm grateful for: _____

Today, I forgive myself for: _____

★ ★ **First, WIN at writing! Do your check-out and reward yourself!** ★ ★

TODAY'S ACTIVITY TO WIN: THINK ABOUT YOUR BRANDING

Your author brand is important to keep in mind any time you are presenting yourself online. You'll also have it in mind when you work on your website, hop on social media, or answer emails. You may have more than one brand if you plan to work on different areas of writing.

For instance, my brand for my nonfiction work is to help other writers and build community.

My brand for my fiction is to explore the fabric of the universe and how people protect the ones they love.

But I don't want to reinvent the wheel. Of course, my brand will be unique to me, but there are other authors, further along in their careers, who have a brand that I want to emulate. I have cbosen a brand mentor and when career decisions arise, I often question, "What would my brand mentor do?" When you have someone specific in mind, this is a very helpful exercise.

My brand mentor is someone who publishes both in fiction and non-fiction and has a very thoughtful and kind online presence. Her achievements inspire me to work forward on my own projects and show me that my goals can be met and exceeded.

If you don't already have someone in mind whose career you'd like to emulate, take some time and do some research. Is there someone with an online presence who writes in all the genres you'd like to write in and has a wide fan base? Can you find someone who presents themselves online in the way you imagine you'd like to? You may find more than one person to be a brand mentor for you.

Your brand mentor will have much in common with you—your output ability, your genre, the way you communicate with your fans. Once you have that person in mind, take a look at all their products, website, and social media interactions. Use their brand as a talisman for your own brand. Of course, your brand will be unique to you, but following in someone's footsteps can make the decision-making process much simpler.

Who is your brand mentor?

Author's Thank You Note: Thank you to author **Erica Orloff** for being the best mentor an author could ever have–I lean on you more than you could possibly know!

Day 24

BONUS WIN: Do a deep dive into your brand mentor's techniques. Discover how they nurture their brand, their writing, their fans. Go back to your Idea Orchard and one and five-year plans and consider whether you want to tweak anything.

DONE LIST:

1. _____
2. _____
3. _____

CHECK-OUT:

Today's creative process flowed for me:

Not flowed **0 1 2 3 4 5 6 7 8 9 10** Totally flowed

Review your writing plans for tomorrow and get psyched for day nineteen of writing!

MY PLAN FOR NEXT WRITING BLOCK:

Date: _____

Time: _____

TO-DOS I WILL ACCOMPLISH:

1. _____ 3. _____
2. _____ 4. _____

TOOLS I PLAN TO USE IF I BECOME FRUSTRATED:

1. _____ 3. _____
2. _____ 4. _____

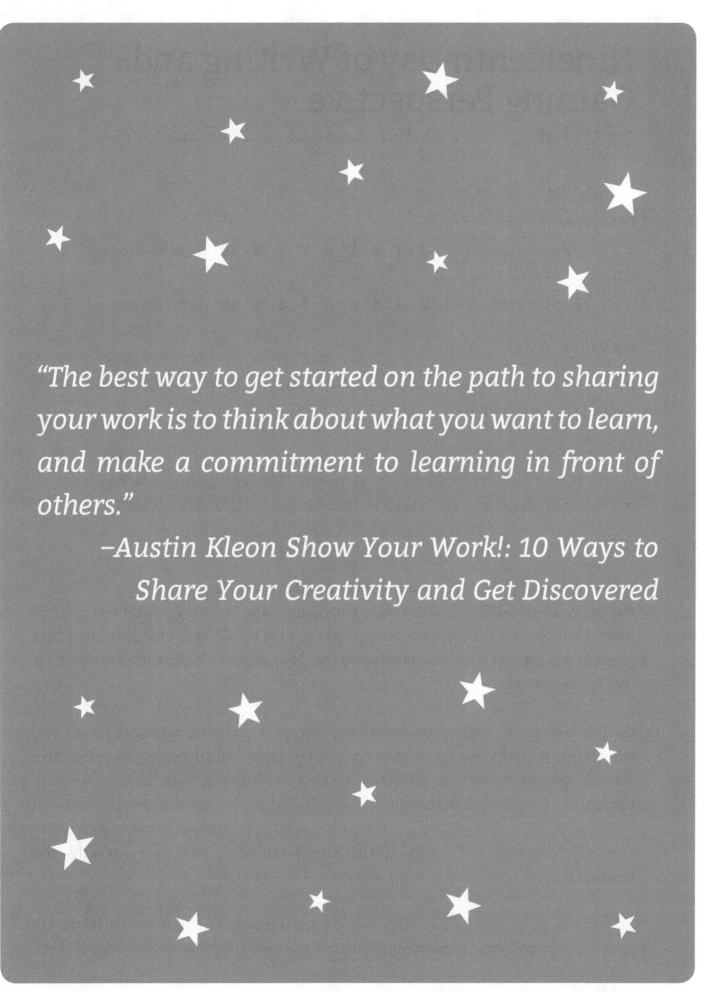

"The best way to get started on the path to sharing your work is to think about what you want to learn, and make a commitment to learning in front of others."

—Austin Kleon Show Your Work!: 10 Ways to Share Your Creativity and Get Discovered

Nineteenth Day of Writing and Gaining Perspective

Day 25 Tasks: Write and think about how to get distance from your creation!

CHECK-IN:

I'm excited to create:

      Not excited   **0 1 2 3 4 5 6 7 8 9 10**   Totally excited

I'm focused today:

      Not focused   **0 1 2 3 4 5 6 7 8 9 10**   Totally focused

My Writing WHY: _____

Today, I'm grateful for: _____

Today, I forgive myself for: _____

Make sure to WIN at writing for the day and write your done list and plan for next time in the check-out! Reward yourself on another win!

TODAY'S ACTIVITY TO WIN: GAIN PERSPECTIVE

Finding context is difficult while you're entrenched in your writing. But if you can find some distance to try to experience your project as a fan would, that's ideal. To know how your fan will interact with your product so that you can make it the best experience for that fan as you can.

Gaining perspective means you know your strengths and weaknesses. It means you see your story clearly and know what you need to revise. Most people gain perspective through time away from the project, self-reflection, feedback from critique partners/ editors, or a combination of those.

Critiquing someone else's work also gives you clarity on your own strengths and weaknesses.

This brings us to how to add other writers and authors into your—some might say network—I'm going to say **community**. This is the third time that we've waded into the waters of building your writing support system. We keep circling back around because building your community is the best way to have access to what you need to get to the next level in your career. To WIN at your writing endeavors.

As I've mentioned before, the best way to begin this process is to ask what you can do for other writers. "What can I do for you?" seems counterintuitive when you're hoping that fellow writers would help you, but when you build up your community, you help yourself. Why? Because you're not looking for a one-off. You're not looking for someone to tell you what's wrong with this one chapter or this one project. Remember your five-year goals? You're looking for support and perspective for what you're working on right now, but also for the long haul—for all the future projects you may dream up.

Where you can find your community: local, regional, and national writers' organizations; conferences; online writing groups/communities, and all the other places you've already brainstormed in earlier sections. There are great places online to get critiques from other writers—all you have to do is search for them.

The goal is for you to have a plan in place to gain perspective on your writing when you are ready for this step, by having someone lined up to give you feedback.

I like to get feedback from people with different strengths than me. If I've asked someone for a critique, then that person can assume that I think they are brilliant at one or more areas of writing. Maybe they excel at worldbuilding or dialog or building tension. Whether they know it or not, I am specifically looking at parts of their feedback for guidance.

I have an extensive list of critique partners and editors I lean on. But that wasn't always the case. I started out by offering to critique everyone else's manuscripts. This helped me learn about my own writing, because it was easier for me to see my own weaknesses in others' writing. It also taught me who might be a good fit to critique my work. And when you continually pay it forward, people are really happy to return the favor and do critiques for you.

Prepare for sharing this current manuscript with others, whether you are starting to find critiquers, planning to hire an editor, or you already have your team lined up!

When I am ready to have someone critique my work, this is my plan:

1. _____

2. _____

3. _____

4. _____

5. _____

6. _____

7. _____

8. _____

9. _____

10. _____

11. _____

12. _____

13. _____

14. _____

BONUS WIN: Seeing your manuscript in different ways can give you amazing perspective. Read your manuscript like a reader. Plunk it into Vellum (it's free to try out) or a pdf to read on your e-reader and experience it like a fan. Read it aloud, or have your computer read it to you. Every time you experience your project in a different way than in your word processor, you see it in a different light.

DONE LIST:

1. _____

2. _____

3. _____

CHECK-OUT:

Today's creative process flowed for me:

Not flowed **0 1 2 3 4 5 6 7 8 9 10** Totally flowed

Review your writing plans for tomorrow
and get psyched for **day twenty of writing!**

MY PLAN FOR NEXT WRITING BLOCK:

Date: _____

Time: _____

TO-DOS I WILL ACCOMPLISH:

1. _____   3. _____

2. _____   4. _____

TOOLS I PLAN TO USE IF I BECOME FRUSTRATED:

1. _____   3. _____

2. _____   4. _____

Twentieth Day of Writing and Exploring Strengths and Weaknesses

Day 26 Tasks: Write and think about what makes you an awesome author!

CHECK-IN:

I'm excited to create:

Not excited **0 1 2 3 4 5 6 7 8 9 10** Totally excited

I'm focused today:

Not focused **0 1 2 3 4 5 6 7 8 9 10** Totally focused

My Writing WHY: _____

Today, I'm grateful for: _____

Today, I forgive myself for: _____

★ **Great job winning your writing today!** ★
★ **Check out and reward yourself!** ★

TODAY'S ACTIVITY TO WIN: EXPLORING STRENGTHS AND WEAKNESSES

On Worksheet Thirteen, we touched on your writing strengths for a moment. But it's important to go a bit deeper. By now you've been writing for twenty days. You know what things come easy, and you probably have an idea of what is harder.
Brainstorm your strengths and weaknesses as a starting off point.

My Writing Strengths:

_____

_____

_____

_____

_____

_____

_____

_____

_____

My Writing Weaknesses:

_____

_____

_____

_____

_____

_____

_____

_____

_____

_____

Most writers spend a lot of time shoring up their weaknesses and do tons of research learning to do the things that don't necessarily come naturally.

However, a few times I've come across an alternate idea. Cheryl Klein touched upon it in her book, Second Sight, and Becca Syme mentioned something similar in her book Dear Writer, You Need to Quit.

I'm paraphrasing and interpreting here, but the idea is that fans will excuse some faults if you are brilliant at a big aspect of writing. The books that fans want to rip through aren't always without fault. But there is magic in those books, because the author is crazy good at one or more aspects of writing, whether it is driving the action or making the reader feel like they are in the shoes of the character or something else.

So instead of focusing on how you can reduce your weaknesses as an author, I want you to first focus on how to magnify your strengths.

And, I want you to let go of the idea that you will become perfect at every aspect of writing or that your product will be perfect. When we have this goal, even subconsciously, it is a huge hurdle to get over.

Of course, we all want to be brilliant at everything about writing. But how much fun is it to get better at the things we're already confident doing? So. Much. Fun.

Come up with a plan to really dive into your strengths as a writer. Whether it is studying craft books, using writing prompts to practice, or simply letting yourself experiment with your strengths to the max, switching your focus on your strengths instead of your weaknesses will bring new life to your project.

My plan for magnifying my strengths:

_____

_____

_____

_____

_____

_____

_____

_____

_____

_____

_____

_____

_____

_____

_____

Really embrace your strengths and allow them to bring you confidence when you sit down to write!

BONUS WIN: Take a look at Cheryl Klein's book, The Magic Words. This book is specifically geared toward YA and kidlit writers, but it has wonderful activities that would benefit and inspire all writers!

DONE LIST:

1. _____

2. _____

3. _____

CHECK-OUT:

Today's creative process flowed for me:

Not flowed **0 1 2 3 4 5 6 7 8 9 10** Totally flowed

**Review your writing plans for tomorrow
and get psyched for day twenty-one of writing!**

MY PLAN FOR NEXT WRITING BLOCK:

Date: _____

Time: _____

TO-DOS I WILL ACCOMPLISH:

1. _____ 3. _____

2. _____ 4. _____

TOOLS I PLAN TO USE IF I BECOME FRUSTRATED:

1. _____ 3. _____

2. _____ 4. _____

Twenty-first Day of Writing and Staying on Target

Day 27 Tasks: Write and try to avoid the bling!

CHECK-IN:

I'm excited to create:

Not excited   **0 1 2 3 4 5 6 7 8 9 10**   Totally excited

I'm focused today:

Not focused   **0 1 2 3 4 5 6 7 8 9 10**   Totally focused

My Writing WHY: _____

Today, I'm grateful for: _____

Today, I forgive myself for: _____

Did you WIN your writing for the day?! Yay! Check out and reward yourself

Twenty-one days of doing something creates a habit—so go you! You've WON! You've created a sustainable writing habit and momentum toward accomplishing your goals!

TODAY'S ACTIVITY TO WIN: STAY ON TARGET

Sometimes we get distracted by the shiny new ideas in our head.

New ideas are beautiful things and we have a place to keep them safe until we're ready to work on them. Add them to your Idea Orchard, and keep plugging away at your current creative work.

But that can be hard. We don't always want to stick with what we're working on. Because writing gets hard. Maybe we hit a murky middle, write ourselves into a corner, or maybe it's time to revise and that's daunting.

When the going gets tough in our current project, it's tempting to start something brand new. It's important to resist this feeling and stay the course. There is tremendous value in finishing a project. In writing a project all the way to the end. And then getting feedback and revising it until we're happy.

If your pattern is to abandon projects, it is important to dig in and find out why. And it's important to find support to get you past whatever hurdle you're getting stuck on. We've talked about our fears and barriers throughout this workbook. If you drop projects while still drafting, then find a mentor for plotting stories. If you drop projects before revision, then find a mentor for revision. If you drop projects before getting critiques, then find a mentor to help you through getting feedback.

A mentor doesn't have to be a person. It can be a craft book, online workshop, or a video. The most important thing is that you recognize that you are having a negative reaction to a part of the process that is keeping you from completing your goals. Re-do Worksheet Seven and take a look at the fears that are getting in your way.

Revisit your goals and your **why.**

And, if you have dropped one project and picked up a new one, consider looking at Section Thirty-One: When You've Missed a Day. Because even though you might be keeping up the habit of writing (GO YOU!), you've missed a day of working toward the goal that you pledged to yourself.

Author's Thank You Note: Thank you to **Charlotte Sheer** for showing me how to keep that momentum going. I'm in awe of your productivity and positive perseverance through this crazy publishing business!

BONUS WIN: Check out The Well-Storied Podcast with Kristen Kieffer, Episode #95: *How to Overcome Shiny New Idea Syndrome & Find Writing Focus*. She reassures us with what we already know—that producing creative products means a lot of hard work. The good news is that you are already far into doing the work! Trust your process!

DONE LIST:

1. _____   3. _____

2. _____

CHECK-OUT:

Today's creative process flowed for me:

Not flowed   **0 1 2 3 4 5 6 7 8 9 10**   Totally flowed

Review your writing plans for tomorrow
and get psyched for **day twenty-one of writing!**

MY PLAN FOR NEXT WRITING BLOCK:

Date: _____

Time: _____

TO-DOS I WILL ACCOMPLISH:

1. _____   3. _____

2. _____   4. _____

TOOLS I PLAN TO USE IF I BECOME FRUSTRATED:

1. _____   3. _____

2. _____   4. _____

"People who want to write either do it or they don't. At last, I began to say that my most important talent – or habit – was persistence. Without it, I would have given up writing long before I finished my first novel. It's amazing what we can do if we simply refuse to give up."

–Octavia E. Butler

Twenty-second Day of Writing and Being Vulnerable

Day 28 Tasks: Write! And finding strength in being vulnerable.

CHECK-IN:

I'm excited to create:

Not excited **0 1 2 3 4 5 6 7 8 9 10** Totally excited

I'm focused today:

Not focused **0 1 2 3 4 5 6 7 8 9 10** Totally focused

My Writing WHY: _____

Today, I'm grateful for: _____

Today, I forgive myself for: _____

Go write, so you can WIN the day! Then celebrate! You have built up so much momentum during this month—go you!

TODAY'S ACTIVITY TO WIN: BEING VULNERABLE

Whether you're trading manuscripts with a critique partner, working with an editor, submitting to agents or editors, or putting your work out into the world, you are going to make yourself vulnerable.

And that can be hard.

You'll get feedback. And discover your work wasn't conveying what you thought it was when you were creating it. Some people like your work and others don't.
You're going to risk things. You're going to fail. It's going to feel awful. You're going to question why you are creating things and putting them into the world. You're going to want to hide. You're going to want to stop.

First, forgive yourself for making yourself vulnerable. Then think about everything you have to be grateful for. Pull out your toolboxes of tools. The big one.

Consider the following tools as well:

- Checking out how your brand mentor handles the naysayers or haters.
- Talking to other writers in your community for empathy and support.
- Taking some time off to gain perspective.
- Working on a shiny new idea!
- Reviewing your five-year goals and see how much closer you are at reaching them. As others are tearing you down, you are making headway!
- Knowing that if you don't risk anything you won't get any big wins. So go after the big wins and let go of the tough stuff!

And then know that we grow the most when we risk. When we are honest and make real connections in the world. When we make mistakes and feel like we stumble and fall. There is no way around the feelings we have when we are vulnerable—we have to live through them.

The most important thing is that you don't let the fear of being vulnerable keep you from putting your creative work into the world.

You can do this.

And you don't have to do it alone. You can always reach out to other authors who know how you are feeling. You can reach out to me. Just visit heatherkellyauthor.com and drop me an email!

BONUS WIN: Check out Brene Brown's TED Talk *Why Your Critics Aren't The Ones Who Count*. It's worth it to do a deep dive into more Brene Brown TED Talks! She's inspirational, raw, and amazing.

BONUS BONUS WIN: Watch Cara E. Yar Khan in her TED Talk, *The Beautiful Balance Between Courage and Fear*, and take inspiration from her story.

DONE LIST:

1. _____   3. _____

2. _____

CHECK-OUT:

Today's creative process flowed for me:

Not flowed **0 1 2 3 4 5 6 7 8 9 10** Totally flowed

Today's creative process flowed for me:

Not flowed **0 1 2 3 4 5 6 7 8 9 10** Totally flowed

Review your writing plans for tomorrow
and get psyched for **day twenty-two of writing!**

MY PLAN FOR NEXT WRITING BLOCK:

Date: _____

Time: _____

TO-DOS I WILL ACCOMPLISH:

1. _____   3. _____

2. _____   4. _____

TOOLS I PLAN TO USE IF I BECOME FRUSTRATED:

1. _____   3. _____

2. _____   4. _____

"If there's a book you really want to read, but it hasn't been written yet, then you must write it."

–Toni Morrison

Twenty-third Day of Writing and Working in the World of Social Media

Day 29 Tasks: Write and be mindful of social media.

CHECK-IN:

I'm excited to create:

Not excited **0 1 2 3 4 5 6 7 8 9 10** Totally excited

I'm focused today:

Not focused **0 1 2 3 4 5 6 7 8 9 10** Totally focused

My Writing WHY: _____

Today, I'm grateful for: _____

Today, I forgive myself for: _____

TODAY'S ACTIVITY TO WIN: BE SOCIAL MEDIA SAVVY

Social media can be a great way to connect and build your community, but it can also be a distraction. And it can be an issue when we see other people's successes while we're on our own trajectory.

Sometimes we feel that we are in competition with every other writer out there. But this perspective can isolate us and make us feel depressed. It can feel like there are less pieces of the pie for ourselves.

I like the perspective of one author on a romance panel at the James River Writer's Conference— "a high tide lifts all boats."

You are only actually competing with one person—yourself. And if this workbook is any indication, you're winning!

As Anne Lamott has said, "Never compare your insides to everyone else's outsides," which is what we are apt to do when we plug in and look at what everyone else is presenting to the world.

Social media can also be a big time-suck, unless we have a reason for being there that lines up with our values and goals.

Social media also reminds us that if we publish books, traditionally or independently, we have to manage the marketing ourselves; we have to have a public persona.

But by this point, you have the tools and tricks to present your brand to the world, and not get caught up in comparisons. You know what direction you're going in and how to get there. You've proven through this workbook that you have the dedication and desire to work through barriers, whether they are internal or external.

BONUS WIN: Check out Chimamanda Ngozi Adichie's TED Talk *The Danger of a Single Story*. Remember that you are writing things that only you can write. And that you can help others who have their stor y to tell as well.

Author's Thank You Note: Thank you to **Josh Funk** for showing professionalism at every turn--I've learned so much from your ability to revise without an ego and the masterful way you maneuver through social media to reach your fans!

CHECK-OUT:

Today's creative process flowed for me:

Not flowed **0 1 2 3 4 5 6 7 8 9 10** Totally flowed

GREAT JOB WINNING THE DAY!
★ Review your writing plans for tomorrow ★
and get psyched for **day twenty-three of writing!**

MY PLAN FOR NEXT WRITING BLOCK:

Date: _____

Time: _____

TO-DOS I WILL ACCOMPLISH:

1. _____   3. _____

2. _____   4. _____

TOOLS I PLAN TO USE IF I BECOME FRUSTRATED:

1. _____   3. _____

2. _____   4. _____

Day Thirty and Every Day After: What I Need Now

Day 30 Task: Write and determine What I Need (WIN)

CHECK-IN:

I'm excited to create:

Not excited **0 1 2 3 4 5 6 7 8 9 10** Totally excited

I'm focused today:

Not focused **0 1 2 3 4 5 6 7 8 9 10** Totally focused

My Writing WHY: _____

Today, I'm grateful for: _____

Today, I forgive myself for: _____

Now that you've completed this workbook and done all the activities in it, you have a strong sense of who you are, what you write, where you want to spend your time, your goals, and how to make small changes to get there.

The work isn't done. But hopefully you're feeling happier and more fulfilled by your creative life. You're in a different place than you were when you started this journey.

There's value in AGAIN. Doing the workbook again, doing the pages again, watching and listening to the resources again. It's why there are copies of the worksheets in the Appendix.

There is also value in MORE. Listen to more podcasts by people mentioned in this workbook. Watch more TED Talks queued up when you watch the suggested ones. Read more craft books.

Perhaps the most value is in figuring out what you need, right now, to get you to the next level in your career.

Every writer always needs something. This workbook supplied you with some of the things each day, that maybe you needed. But only you truly know what you need. The good news is that whatever you need, help is out there for you. You just have to know how to ask for it or connect yourself to it.

1. Don't re-invent the wheel. If you have a problem with something, chances are someone else has had that same problem. And already discovered a solution. Find them. See if their solution is your solution.

2. Find an expert. You can always find that expert you need and listen to their words of wisdom. Both one and two are tenants we delved into during our deeper dives. Hopefully, through the BONUS WINS, you discovered experts to help you solve problems you come across.

3. Ask for help—and build your community. A community is built one person at a time. If you are willing to put yourself out there and ask what you can do for others, then when you need help, you'll have it!

4. Remove barriers. Use tools and practice to help flip the emotions attached to creating—the psychological barriers. Use craft books and mentors to help reduce any knowledge barriers.

5. Make writing a habit. You can accomplish any goal when you are willing to do the hard work.

CONGRATULATIONS ON WINNING YOUR 30 DAY JUMPSTART!

Don't stop now: Use the following worksheet to create a writing log going forward, and the worksheets in the Appendix to redo exercises from this workbook, as needed.

BONUS WIN: Check out Amanda Palmer's TED Talk *The Art of Asking*. Don't ever be afraid to ask for what you need to WIN your writing goals!

Worksheet 19: WIN at Writing Blueprint

Day: _____

My writing goal:

_____

_____

_____

_____

_____

_____

_____

My deep dive/filling of the creative well:

_____

_____

_____

_____

_____

_____

_____

_____

What I need now and how I'm going to get it:

_____

_____

_____

_____

_____

_____

_____

DONE LIST:

1. _____

2. _____

3. _____

CHECK-OUT:

Today's creative process flowed for me:

Not flowed   **0 1 2 3 4 5 6 7 8 9 10**   Totally flowed

**Review your writing plans for tomorrow
and get psyched for more writing!**

MY PLAN FOR NEXT WRITING BLOCK:

Date: _____

Time: _____

TO-DOS I WILL ACCOMPLISH:

1. _____   3. _____

2. _____   4. _____

TOOLS I PLAN TO USE IF I BECOME FRUSTRATED:

1. _____   3. _____

2. _____   4. _____

Thirty-one: When You've Missed A Day

We give ourselves grace for missing our planned writing day.

We give ourselves grace for missing our planned writing day.

You've hit a day when you couldn't or didn't want to follow through on your pledge to your creative self.

- **That's okay.**
- **Practice kindness with yourself.**
- **Sometimes life happens.**

But, if it wasn't life that happened; if it was something about your to-do list or schedule or your writing that made you skip today, let's process that.

Follow the Flowchart on the next worksheet to help you get back on track, and to point you to the direction of where you can find help in this manual.

Today's WIN: Search for and check out Tim Urban's very funny TED Talk *Inside the Mind of a Master Procrastinator!*

 I'm practicing kindness with myself for missing a day.
Knowing why, I know how to get back on track.

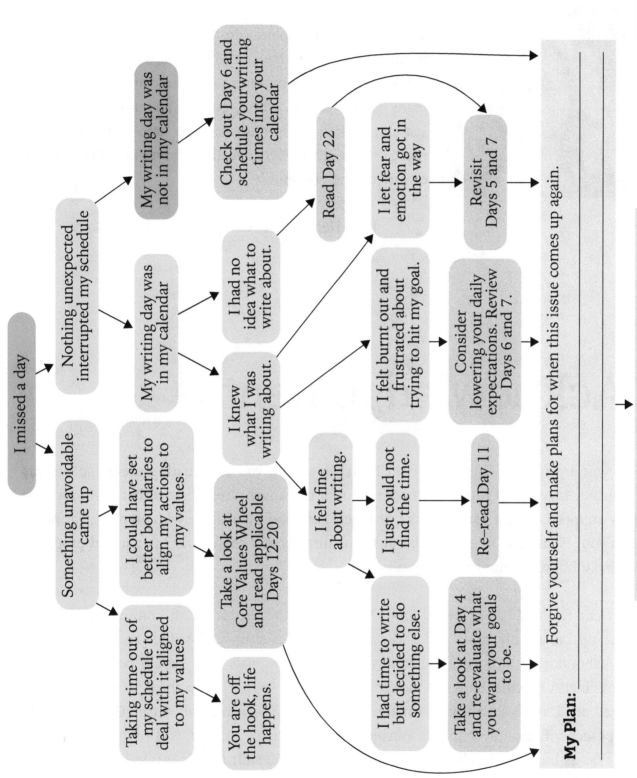

About the Author

Heather Kelly explores the fabric of the universe through writing MG, YA, and everything in between. She founded the Writers' Loft community in Sherborn, MA and wears many hats—teacher, editor, author, director. She's always searching for (and finding) ways to help authors become more prolific storytellers. Heather thrives on collaboration, creativity, and community.

Find Heather on Twitter at @HeatherGKelly

Acknowledgements

If you are reading this workbook, I wish to thank you for trusting me to go on this journey together. If you got something out of this adventure, please either pay it forward by supporting your local authors or reach back and help those who aren't as far along as you. Please feel free to reach out to me directly and share your insight and progress! Email: hegkelly+jumpstart@gmail.com

I want to thank every writer and illustrator in the Writers' Loft community. You lift me up on a daily basis and show me what is creatively possible. You are my best collaborators, colleagues, and cohorts. Without you, this book would never have been possible. A specific thanks to the cheerleading and support from the Self/Indie Group at the Loft: Dave Pasquantonio, Kristen Wixted, Julie Morganlender, Susan Catalano, Jodie Apeseche, Elana Varon, Louis Panagotopulos, Michael McAfee, and John David Ferrer. As far as building this book, thank you to Bob Thibeault for his masterful and creative ways! Thank you all and **keep winning!**

Appendix

Worksheet 1: WIN at Creating Your Idea Orchard

Worksheet 2: WIN at Brainstorming the Future

Worksheet 3: WIN at Your Mission

Worksheet 4: WIN at Creating Goals

Worksheet 5: WIN at Breaking Goals into Doable Steps

Worksheet 6: WIN at Saying YES!

Worksheet 7: WIN at Defeating Fears!

Worksheet 8: WIN at Gratefulness and Forgiveness

Worksheet 9: WIN at To-Do Listing

Worksheet 10: WIN at Building a Toolbox of Big Tools

Worksheet 11: WIN at Building Your Toolbox of in-the Moment (Small) Tools

Worksheet 12: WIN at Stocking Toolboxes

Worksheet 13: WIN at Strategies

Worksheet 14: WIN at Workflow

Worksheet 15: WIN at Tracking Time

Worksheet 16: WIN at Aligning My Values

Worksheet 17: Win the Financial Audit

Worksheet 18: WIN at Building My Community

Worksheet 19: WIN at Writing Blueprint

Worksheet 20: WIN at Following the Missed Day Flowchart

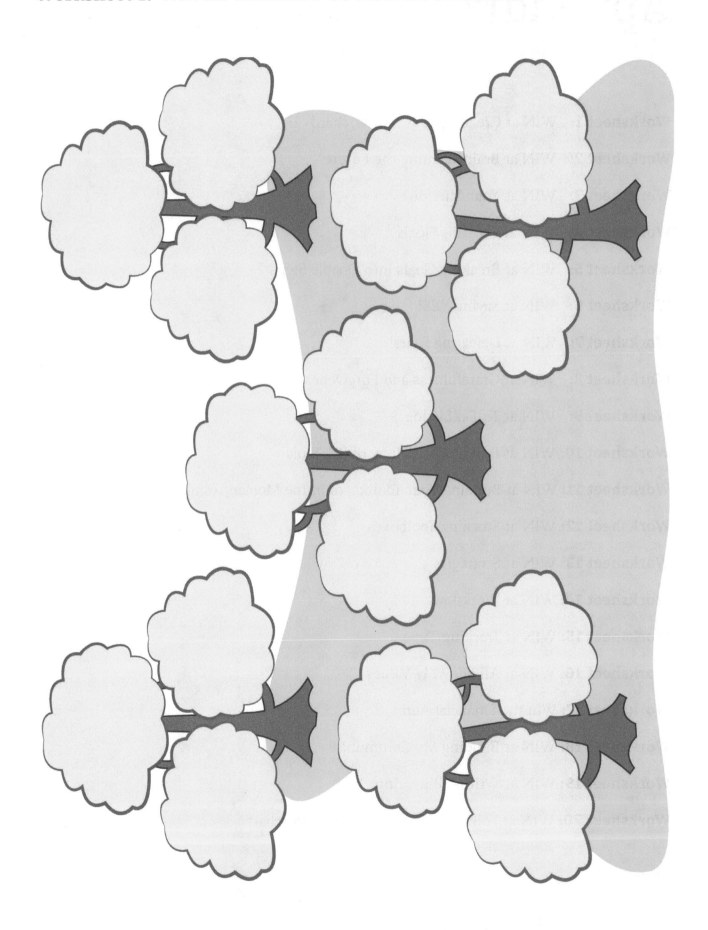

Worksheet 2: WIN AT BRAINSTORMING THE FUTURE

Brainstorm writing-related projects you're thinking about doing in the next five years here.

Now, think in terms of the next 365 days. What writing-related projects do you want to take on sooner rather than later?

Worksheet 3: WIN AT YOUR MISSION

Brainstorm your mission(s) here. Write down everything that comes to mind about you and your writing:

Turn your mission into a statement, that you can use as a bio or a statement that encapsulates your writing career.

_____

_____

_____

_____

_____

_____

_____

_____

_____

Worksheet 4: WIN AT CREATING GOALS

Goal: _____

_____

Why: _____

_____

_____

Goal: _____

_____

Why: _____

_____

_____

Goal: _____

_____

Why: _____

_____

_____

Goal: _____

_____

Why: _____

_____

_____

Goal: _____

_____

Why: _____

_____

Goal: _____

_____

Why: _____

_____

Worksheet 5: WIN AT BREAKING GOALS INTO DOABLE STEPS

Goal: _____

_____

Steps: _____

_____

_____

_____

_____

_____

_____

Goal: _____

_____

Steps: _____

_____

_____

_____

_____

_____

_____

Goal: _____

_____

Steps: _____

_____

_____

_____

_____

_____

_____

Worksheet 6: WIN AT SAYING YES!

Name of my product:

_____

_____

One sentence about my product (a pitch):

_____

_____

_____

_____

_____

Why I want to create this product right now:

_____

_____

_____

_____

_____

_____

_____

My goal for completion of this project (time frame):

_____

_____

The steps I'm taking to complete this project:

1. _____   6. _____

   _____   _____

2. _____   7. _____

   _____   _____

3. _____   8. _____

   _____   _____

4. _____   9. _____

   _____   _____

5. _____   10. _____

   _____   _____

Worksheet 7: WIN AT DEFEATING FEARS

Fear: _____

_____

Evidence or But: _____

_____

Fear: _____

_____

Evidence or But: _____

_____

Fear: _____

_____

Evidence or But: _____

_____

Fear: _____

_____

Evidence or But: _____

_____

Fear: _____

_____

Evidence or But: _____

_____

Fear: _____

_____

Evidence or But: _____

_____

Worksheet 8: WIN AT DEFEATING FEARS

Make a list here of some of the things you are grateful for today:

_____

_____

_____

_____

_____

_____

_____

_____

_____

_____

_____

What do you forgive yourself for?

_____

_____

_____

_____

_____

_____

_____

_____

_____

_____

_____

_____

Worksheet 9: WIN AT TO-DO LISTING

Name of my project: _____

_____

List of to-dos:

_____	_____
_____	_____
_____	_____
_____	_____
_____	_____
_____	_____
_____	_____
_____	_____
_____	_____
_____	_____
_____	_____
_____	_____
_____	_____
_____	_____
_____	_____
_____	_____
_____	_____
_____	_____

Worksheet 10: WIN AT BUILDING A TOOLBOX OF BIG TOOLS

- Journaling
- Exercising/working out/being on a sports team
- Joining an advocacy group or religious center
- Reading/listening to an audio book
- Socializing
- Watching TV/a movie
- Talking to a friend/family member
- Caring for a pet
- Being creative in other ways: drawing, photography, knitting, baking
- Creating a list of to-dos and getting them done
- Singing/playing musical instruments
- Walking

- Playing a game with others or alone
- Being outside
- Talking with a therapist/religious official
- Going to group therapy
- Going to the chiropractor/masseuse
- Going shopping
- Watching TED Talks
- Cooking
- Volunteering
- Meditating
- Going away on vacation!
- Listening to music
- Dancing
- Listening to a podcast

Others tools that aren't on the list that you want to use when the going gets tough:

_____   _____

_____   _____

_____   _____

_____   _____

_____   _____

Now, list your top five tools that resonate with you.

Top Five Big Tools:

1. _____
2. _____
3. _____
4. _____
5. _____

Worksheet 11:
WIN AT BUILDING YOUR TOOLBOX of IN–THE MOMENT (small) TOOLS

- Reaching out to a writing partner
- Playing a five-minute game on your phone/computer/tablet
- Taking a brief walk
- Watching a short video
- Listening to music
- Getting a drink
- Zoning out for ten minutes
- Visualizing your product finished
- Eating—because maybe your brain is hungry!
- Listening to a short podcast
- Brainstorming what comes next

Add your own tools here:

1. _____
2. _____
3. _____
4. _____
5. _____

Now, list your top five tools that resonate with you.

Top Five Small Tools:

1. _____
2. _____
3. _____
4. _____
5. _____

My Big Toolbox to Fill My Emotional Well:

1. _____
2. _____
3. _____
4. _____
5. _____

My Small Toolbox to Use in the Moment:

1. _____
2. _____
3. _____
4. _____
5. _____

Worksheet 13: WIN AT STRATEGIES

My writing strengths:

_____

_____

_____

_____

_____

What time of day do I do my best writing?

_____

What type of environment do I like to create in?

_____

_____

How long do I like to work before taking a break?

_____

_____

If interrupted, can I go back to work?

_____

What other strategies work?

_____

_____

_____

What strategies would I like to try to optimize my writing sessions?

_____

_____

_____

Worksheet 14: WIN AT WORKFLOW

I keep my ideas and notes here:

_____

_____

I keep my outlines here:

_____

_____

I keep my "book bible" (worldbuilding, story notes, etc.) here:

_____

_____

I write my manuscripts using this program:

_____

_____

I keep backups of my manuscripts here:

_____

_____

I keep lists of projects here:

_____

_____

I keep to-do lists and schedules here:

_____

_____

When I send manuscripts for critiques or edits, I name them this way:

_____

_____

Tools and craft guides I keep by my computer in case I need to use them:

_____

_____

Anything else I want to remember about my workflow:

_____

Worksheet 15: WIN AT TIME AUDITING

9:00	1:00	5:00
9:15	1:15	5:15
9:30	1:30	5:30
9:45	1:45	5:45
10:00	2:00	6:00
10:15	2:15	6:15
10:30	2:30	6:30
10:45	2:45	6:45
11:00	3:00	7:00
11:15	3:15	7:15
11:30	3:30	7:30
11:45	3:45	7:45
12:00	4:00	8:00
12:15	4:15	8:15
12:30	4:30	8:30
12:45	4:45	8:45

©2020 Pocket Moon Press • heatherkellyauthor.com

Worksheet 16: WIN at Aligning My Values

My priorities:

1. _____
2. _____
3. _____
4. _____
5. _____

Things I want to say yes to, that align with my values:

1. _____
2. _____
3. _____
4. _____
5. _____

Things I want to set boundaries around/say no to:

1. _____
2. _____
3. _____
4. _____
5. _____

Itemize and total your last month's expenses. Group things together, so if you visit Starbucks fifteen times, enter that total on a line in Food and Drink Expenses as one total. Then total up each block.

Month:

Food and Drink Expenses

			Total:

Clothing Expenses

			Total:

Utility Expenses (rent/mortgate/utilites)

			Total:

Technology Expenses (cable, phones)

			Total:

Health Expenses

			Total:

Entertainment and Fun Expenses

			Total:

Travel

			Total:

Business Expenses

			Total:

Other

			Total:

Brainstorm who can help you in each area of community. If you need to find someone to fit a category, brainstorm where you might connect with them.

1. Knowledge

2. Emotional Support

3. Feedback

4. Shared Resources

5. Accountability

Worksheet 19: WIN at Writing Blueprint

Day: _____

My writing goal: _____

_____

CHECK-IN:

I'm excited to create:

      Not excited   **0 1 2 3 4 5 6 7 8 9 10** Totally excited

I'm focused today:

      Not focused   **0 1 2 3 4 5 6 7 8 9 10** Totally focused

My Writing WHY: _____

Today, I'm grateful for: _____

Today, I forgive myself for: _____

✦ Yay! You WON the day! ✦

DONE LIST:

1. _____

2. _____

3. _____

CHECK-OUT:

Today's creative process flowed for me:

      Not flowed   **0 1 2 3 4 5 6 7 8 9 10** Totally flowed

**Review your writing plans for tomorrow
and get psyched for day _____ of writing!**

MY PLAN FOR NEXT WRITING BLOCK:

Date: _____

Time: _____

TO-DOS I WILL ACCOMPLISH:

_____   _____

_____   _____

_____   _____

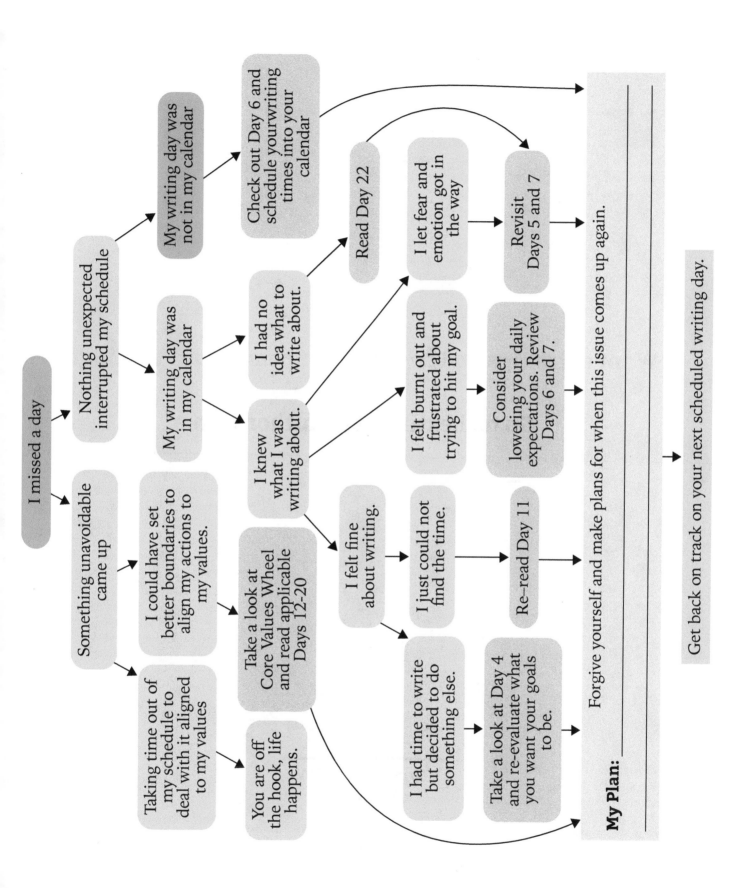

Want extra tips and tricks to jumpstart your writing?

Go to: heatherkellyauthor.com

*Creatively WIN
Workbook*